Every Path Leads Home:

Opening to Your Spiritual Journey

By

Wayne Holmes

2014

Religious Recovery Press

Every Path Leads Home: Opening to Your Spiritual Journey
Copyright © 2014 by Wayne Holmes
All rights reserved.
ISBN 978-0-9898681-0-5
Published by Religious Recovery Press
Liberty Township, Ohio

Book Design by Fred Martens, Martensart.com
Cover Photo by Lisa Gerard
Cover Design by Fred Martens, Martensart.com

Dedicated to the healing and recovery
of those who have been hurt, disappointed,
or abused by religion
or the religious.

Every Path Leads Home:

Opening to Your Spiritual Journey

Chapter 1

RELIGIOUS DIFFERENCES

"Like the bee, gathering honey from different flowers, the wise man accepts the essence of different scriptures and sees only the good in all religions."

–Srimad Bhagavatam

spiritual text of Hinduism

DEAR READER

In ancient times, a traveler asking, "Which road leads to Rome?" might well receive a reply worthy of the Scarecrow in *The Wizard of Oz:* "The way to your left provides a challenge, but the inns along the way are friendly," followed by, "The road you are on is very pleasant as well, and much shorter," and, "The road through that pass in the hills provides both shade and a cool, swift-running stream from which to drink."

Of course, in *The Wizard of Oz,* the scarecrow has an excuse for his indecision: he doesn't have a brain.

In the case of the pilgrim seeking the road to the most important city in the "known world," the reason for the multiple answers was equally simple: in the Roman Empire, all roads led, directly or indirectly, to that one most important city in the known world.

By proposing that "every path leads home"—meaning that all spiritual paths ultimately lead back to The Divine, some may liken me to the Scarecrow rather than the sensible Roman guide.

But if you will, please give me a moment to explain. If The Divine (God, if you prefer) created all things, how can all things not at some point return to Him? Or, as I prefer to say, how can all beings made in His image, not return home? Doesn't this especially hold true for those religions that teach the existence of a single Divine Being who created a single man and a single woman who then populated the entire planet?

The quintessential belief in nearly all religious experience is that The Divine is Love. Would a Being of ultimate love condemn billions of people because they didn't hold the same religious doctrine? Would He not make a way for everyone on the planet to find their way home?

Many religious leaders and followers will say, "No, there is only one way, it is _____." And, they fill in the blank with whatever religious belief they adhere to—usually their birth religion. How can all of these religions claim exclusiveness to the one and only road to God? How do we pick which one is right, because in choosing one we condemn the others?

If I were God, I would build a structure—much like the Roman architects—to make certain my wayward children eventually found their way back to me. I would create an inner compass, an inner homing device, to guide my children. I would leave nothing to chance. No matter what road they took, it would eventually lead them home.

That's what I would do if I were The Divine Being.

Wayne Holmes

TOXIC RELIGION

"There's only one way to God—and it's my way!"

Every time I hear that claim—in one form or another—the muscles in my stomach tighten, my jaw clenches, and I go on the defensive. Who do the people making this claim think they are?

I was attending the funeral of a close friend when one of her relatives approached me. After introducing ourselves I said, "I'm sorry for your loss. She said thanks, and then asked if I followed the news. Hesitantly I said, "Not too much." Embarrassed by the admission, I feebly added that my wife did, and she kept me informed.

"Would you like to know what's going on?" she asked.

The reaction I described above happened again: stomach muscles tightened, jaw clenched, and I prepared for an attack. Something out of the ordinary was going on. Her serious expression boded evil, doom, and gloom. Not knowing what to say next, I asked her to explain.

"I'll show you," she said.

She walked to her car, retrieved some papers, and handed them to me.

"Read this," she said.

I didn't want them. I had come to mourn my friend, and I didn't want whatever propaganda she was proffering. But, thinking my refusal would seem unkind, I took the material.

As she released the papers she added, "This will explain everything."

"Thanks," I said.

She nodded and walked away.

What is this? I thought to myself. *Did this woman come to grieve the death of a relative or to hand out tracts?*

Later I took time to glance through her information, and it was worse than I expected. The flyer condemned our country for having lost its Christian heritage and the United Nations as ungodly. It condemned other religious belief systems and predicted the end of the world because the rest of the world didn't believe in her professed form of religion.

Of all days to be approached by a religious enthusiast, a day of mourning is one of the worst. Having the papers near me made me nervous and uncomfortable. The scent of evil associated itself with the documents, and I wanted nothing to do with the condemnations they preached.

Frankly, I was angry.

In its purest form religion yields happiness, purpose, love, and serenity. How many religious people do you know who demonstrate those qualities? Speaking about one form of religion, Christianity, I heard someone once say, "The problem with Christians is that I've never met one," which sounds similar to what Gandhi once said: "I like your Christ, I do not like your Christians. Your Christians are so unlike your Christ."

In its toxic form religion produces followers who are judgmental, angry, hateful, fanatical, and miserable. They make the people around them uncomfortable with their smug attitude that says, "I know the answers, and if you'll listen and believe as I believe, you can have them too." I've met my share of toxic Christian believers. But Christians don't have a monopoly on toxic religion. Muslims have followers who believe their faith is the only way home—to Allah. Some insist that Buddha and the path to enlightenment is the only road home—to Nirvana. I've been there. I've been that kind of believer.

I once believed that my form of religious Christian faith was the only right path, the only road home to heaven. That only those who believed in Jesus and followed the "Romans Road to Salvation" [1] or "The Four Spiritual Laws" [2] would be swept away into a heaven paved with streets of gold. I taught, preached, and tried to convert people to my way of thinking. Truth is, it wasn't my way of thinking, but only the doctrine handed down to me by other well-meaning people.

Based on my Christian beliefs, religious zeal was logical and mandatory. The logic went like this: God is love. We are to love everyone. God sent his son to die for our sins. Jesus did that on the cross. We must accept Jesus as our savior. If we refuse, then we lose eternal life with God, and are condemned to an eternity in hell.

If we buy into that belief system, then love demands we do our utmost to save the world by converting everyone outside our little group of co-religionists to our own set of religious beliefs and doctrines. I bought into that, and spent a short time going door-to-door trying to spread salvation. One of my not-the-best-witness experiences came when I knocked on the screen door of an older gentleman. As I peered into the house through the screen door, a man—who looked as if he didn't want to be bothered—descended from the second floor as I gathered my courage. "Can I help you?" he asked from the other side of the screen door.

I was on a mission—a mission to save his soul.

---

1 The "Romans Road to Salvation" presents steps to salvation (Christian) based on Scriptures from the New Testament book of Romans.

2 "The Four Spiritual Laws is a Christian tract created by Campus Crusade for Christ founder Bill Bright. In the tract, Bright presents his four steps to salvation through Jesus.

"If you were to die tonight, do you know where you'd spend eternity?"

I'm not much of a mind reader, but even a novice could see he didn't want to be bothered. He frowned, turned without comment, and proceeded back up the stairs.

Angry that I could be dismissed without so much as a word, I yelled through the screen door, "You can know for certain where you'll spend eternity if you acknowledge you're a sinner, confess your sins, ask Jesus to forgive you, and invite him into your heart!"

There, I got all four points in, even though he didn't hear anything past the first two, I thought. But, I was angry. Furious, in fact.

Why? I wondered. *It shouldn't be like this. I was only trying to help him.*

Young and stupid, I didn't understand that his rejection had hit me personally, as if he were not only rejecting my words, but everything I believed in and stood for. I had come to rescue him—well, not me personally, but Jesus.

I was upset. When he refused my offer of eternal life in the name of my religion, I became the persecutor and eventually I took on the victim role.

I've come to understand a different way. The Buddha said, "When the student is ready, the teacher [or master] will appear." The man wasn't ready to hear my words. Or maybe he had heard the same rhetoric before and had made a decision. Who was I to force my religion upon him or anyone? Who says that Christianity is the right religion—or the only road home?

We've come a long way from the example of the followers of Jesus who told the disciples to go into the world and make disciples—not Christians, but disciples. Strong-arm, guilt-ridden tactics were never commanded, hinted at, or implied. Jesus had a spirituality that was contagious. He never had to advertise to draw a crowd. No Facebook page, no social networking.

The same was true with the early followers. They caught the essence of spirituality and it intimidated the religious rulers, threatening their beliefs, social status, and perhaps most importantly, their income.

The early followers didn't canvas neighborhoods door-to-door promoting their new "religion." They lived in peace and harmony, endeavoring to reproduce in their lives what they learned from their teacher. They followed the essence of what the Buddha taught: when the student is ready, the connection between student and teacher will happen. There was so much religious and political fear and hatred of the new thought system that safety became a priority. To openly profess their beliefs often landed Jesus' followers in jail. For some it cost them their lives.

Spirituality has at times offended the established norms. The religious rulers during the time of Jesus railed against him and plotted his demise. Martin Luther King, Jr.

preached a gospel of love and acceptance—and his appeal was met with hatred, bigotry, violence, and his assassination. Dr. King was a Southern Baptist minister and his message of unconditional love and acceptance of all races, creeds, and colors was a spiritual theme for all people and for all religious traditions. Often those who practice nonviolent forms of protest are subjected to violent forms of treatment, even by religious groups who profess love, forgiveness, and tolerance.

Right vs. Wrong: In my attempts to gain converts, the basic problem was right vs. wrong. I was right, and those who did not believe as I did were wrong. There was no room in my religious world for gray areas. My door-to-door attempts to evangelize the world failed miserably. Taking a cue from one of those obnoxious evangelical tracts you sometimes find left in the buildings of highway rest areas and in public restrooms, I began by asking the question, "If you died today, do you know where you would spend eternity?" Talk about a rude way to be greeted on a Saturday morning! It doesn't get much more offensive than that. Today, I look back over my youthful naiveté with mild amusement.

Perhaps, I sound critical of my fundamentalist religious background. However, over the years I've come to accept and appreciate many aspects of the things I learned. The fundamentalists differ little from other religions in that they mean well but often allow man-made doctrines to supersede the basics of love, gratitude, service, and kindness. When we open our minds to world religions, we often find the same concepts permeate them. For example, consider the golden rule

- **Christianity:** Therefore all things whatsoever ye would that men should do to you, do ye even so to them. (Matthew 7: 12 KJV)
- **Confucianism:** Do not do to others what you would not like yourself. Then there will be no resentment against you, either in the family or in the state. —Analects 12:2
- **Buddhism:** Hurt not others in ways that you yourself would find hurtful. —Udana-Varga 5,1
- **Hinduism:** This is the sum of duty: do naught unto others which would cause you pain if done to you." Mahabharata 5:1517
- **Islam:** "Not one of you is a believer until he loves for his brother what he loves for himself." Islam. Forty Hadith of an-Nawawi 13
- **Judaism:** What is hateful to you, do not do to your fellowman. This is the entire Law; all the rest is commentary. —Talmud, Shabbat 3id
- **Taoism:** Regard your neighbor's gain as your gain, and your neighbor's loss as your own loss. —Tai Shang Kan Yin P'ien

Each of these religions says essentially the same thing, some with a bit different emphasis, but all lead to the same destination. By loving others the way we want to be loved, we fulfill the prime call of religion. When we try to define what loving others looks like, differences arise and we get back into the mode of "I'm right—you're wrong." We think by definition that we can't both be right—or both be wrong. I'm reminded of the poem of the blind men who examined an elephant.

The Blind Men and the Elephant

John Godfrey Saxe (1816-1887)

It was six men of Indostan
To learning much inclined,
Who went to see the Elephant
(Though all of them were blind),
That each by observation
Might satisfy his mind.

The First approached the Elephant,
And happening to fall
Against his broad and sturdy side,
At once began to bawl:
"God bless me! but the Elephant
Is very like a WALL!"

The Second, feeling of the tusk,
Cried, "Ho, what have we here,
So very round and smooth and sharp?
To me 'tis mighty clear
This wonder of an Elephant
Is very like a SPEAR!"

The Third approached the animal,
And happening to take
The squirming trunk within his hands,
Thus boldly up and spake:
"I see," quoth he, "the Elephant
Is very like a SNAKE!"

The Fourth reached out an eager hand,
And felt about the knee
"What most this wondrous beast is like
Is mighty plain," quoth he:
"'Tis clear enough the Elephant
Is very like a TREE!"

The Fifth, who chanced to touch the ear,
Said: "E'en the blindest man
Can tell what this resembles most;
Deny the fact who can,
This marvel of an Elephant
Is very like a FAN!"

The Sixth no sooner had begun
About the beast to grope,
Than seizing on the swinging tail
That fell within his scope,
"I see," quoth he, "the Elephant
Is very like a ROPE!"

And so these men of Indostan
Disputed loud and long,
Each in his own opinion
Exceeding stiff and strong,
Though each was partly in the right,
And all were in the wrong![3]

If the world only had one religion, wouldn't it solve conflicts and prevent wars? How would we go about creating a religion that would satisfy everyone? We can't. Like the blind men in the poem, each religion has its own view of reality and no one can pry them from the truth as they see it. Though the Earth may never have one religion, the world religions can understand we only have one Earth and agree to concentrate on our similarities, learn from one another, and let our differences go.

The great Divine is the elephant: we are but blind mice.

We have not yet explored beyond the little toe of God.

---

3 http://constitution.org/col/blind_men.htm

Chapter 2
RELIGIOUS OR SPIRITUAL?

"The essence of religion:
Fear God and obey God.
The essence of spirituality:
Love The Divine and become
Divine-like."

"I'm Not Religious, But I Am Spiritual."

I've heard that statement expressed by people in different places and situations. What do they mean? Some people use the expression to pacify. For some, the term "spiritual" encompasses a belief in a higher being—called God for most in the Western world. However, they may also be open to other concepts.

Religious or Spiritual: What does it mean?

Following is a sense of what I think people mean when they say to me, "I'm not religious, but I am spiritual."

Religious: I go to religious gatherings, say prayers, listen to music, concentrate on the talk, donate money, but I'm empty inside.

Spiritual: I don't attend religious gatherings. My parents made me when I was a child, but I'm not attending now. Still, I talk to God, I pray in my own way, but I feel there must be more. Even though I don't attend religious gatherings, I'm a good person. I know there's more to life than day-to-day existence, and some day, probably after I retire, I'll work on the spiritual aspect of my life.

Those two definitions are scarcely accurate, but let's begin here. Fed up with religious groups and their rituals, knowing there must be more but unable or unwilling to discover what: this loosely defines what it means to be spiritual but not religious.

Looking For More

The heart hungers for a meaningful existence. "Why am I here?" and "What is my purpose?" are questions we ask in the stillness of life—at times of great loss, but also at times of great gain when everything seems to be working. Even in victory and accomplishment the question of meaning and purpose surfaces like a bobber on a fishing line.

When Traditional Religious Gatherings Aren't Enough

Many people—in fact most people—have found at one time or another the answers they seek through mainstream religions: Buddhism, Hinduism, Judaism, Islam, or Christianity, to name a few. But there are those who no longer feel connected with their birth religion. They seek a deeper understanding. Often this search was created because their birth religion did not answer their questions, and the questions wouldn't go away. This sense of being in a spiritual "no man's land" may have been created through a disagreement with a leader of the religious group. They may have come into conflict with a doctrine.

Whatever the reason, the religious assembly disappointed them, circumstances prohibited further participation, and they felt a sense of having been cast adrift.

Now What?

What would it be like to enter the world without a birth religion? Even people who were born with parents who claimed to be atheists or agnostics are still influenced by the "national" religion. American is considered a Christocentric society. Our Supreme Being we have named "God," and his son, "Jesus." That is not to say that America is solely Christian. America has come more and more to resemble a "Joseph's coat of many colors"—an increasing number of religious traditions living for the most part in harmony.

If we were born in a different nation our birth religion might be Hinduism, Islam, or any number of religions, some well-known and others more obscure. If we could choose the religion we wanted to be born with, what would we choose? Which one is right? Which one will get us to where we want to go—heaven, nirvana, enlightenment? Which will bring us the greatest peace in daily life? Which is the most rewarding, the most fulfilling?

Too Complicated

In lieu of all these questions, some have discarded religious belief. The uncertainty of knowing and the effort to discover leave many deciding not to decide. Let the theologians figure it out, I have better things to do. They depart ways with organized religion with its moral confines and dictates of man-made rules. But even those who "shake the dust of organized religion from their feet" leave with a sense of "there must be more." Later, when asked about their religious heritage, the conversation often goes something like this:

"What church/temple/synagogue/mosque do you go to?"

"I grew up as a _____, but I haven't been going for a while."

"Oh?"

"Yeah, I know I should, but I'm just too busy."

"Do you consider yourself a religious person?"

"Mmm, not really religious, but I am spiritual."

There's that phrase again: "I'm not religious; I'm spiritual." They may go on to discuss how they try to live a good life, follow a set of rules such as the Ten Commandments, are kind to strangers, and so on. Is that what they mean by being spiritual: knowing a moral code and doing their best to live within its boundaries?

For some, however, the word "spiritual" has come to mean more than living by a set of laws. It means connecting with a higher power, living according to the promptings of an inner voice, being open to other forms of religion, and understanding that every path leads home. For them, religion can be useful, but also dangerous. They carry that understanding into their new spirituality as well.

Where Do They Meet?

Jesus, Buddha, and other spiritual leaders were not pastors of religious assemblies. The world was their congregation, nature their choir, and shepherds, tax collectors, and prostitutes their flock. They spoke to those who would listen, never demanding an audience, but never turning anyone away.

The new world religious gatherings often begin in the same way. One gathering I attended shared space with a business that taught pole dancing. During the week, students learned to dance on "stripper poles" and on Sundays people met to draw close to their Higher Power.

Two other gatherings I've attended met in a home that tripled as two churches and a ministry office. Another religious gathering I visited met in a room rented from a moving company. I've also attended and visited other groups that met in more traditional religious buildings—some more elaborate than others.

What Do The Spiritual Gatherings Look Like?

The gatherings—referring to the members and not the buildings—look like plumbers, garbage men, civil servants, teachers, business men and women, housewives and househusbands, students—normal, everyday people. But also the not-so-ordinary—prostitutes, tax evaders, criminals, mentally challenged individuals. The emotional makeup of these gatherings varies. A search for a deeper spirituality draws the crowd, usually by word of mouth. No evangelistic knocking on doors, no "this is the way, walk ye in it" speeches, no talk of hell and damnation. Their doors open to all who come with open minds and hearts that yearn for healing.

Which Gathering Is Right For Me?

The gathering that is right for you is the one that works for you. The following are summaries of my experiences of several gatherings that I've visited and have loosely classified as spiritual as opposed to religious. The list is not complete, and it doesn't include gatherings I've attended in traditional churches (except for two) which have, at times, provided spiritual experiences. The gatherings I've described here, however, are, generally speaking, open to all religions and a variety of lifestyles. I carried on this journey my own tradition as a fundamentalist Christian minister.

Spiritual Gathering 1: The first gathering I attended I could only describe as—according to my fundamentalist beliefs—weird. What I knew as a sermon was called a "talk." What I understood as prayer became "affirmations." What I had called contemplation (a time of quiet reflection) became "meditation," and frequently the meditation involved the playing of a crystal bowl.

I haven't personally experienced "speaking in tongues," but I've heard others do it. In my new religious group, during the crystal bowl meditation, the person playing the bowl went into a trance-like state and chanted in a language that, she explained, was similar to Tibetan. I repeat, "weird" was the word that described it for me. And what I understood to be prophecy, or "a word from the Holy Spirit," was conveyed as a psychic reading—a message from The Divine.

One aspect of the service that didn't resonate strongly with me, considering my conservative roots, was the healing circle. Near the end of the service, we stood, joined hands and, after some opening comments about what we were about to do, spoke the names of loved ones, placing them into the center of the circle. A closing prayer offered the names up to The Divine. We squeezed hands before returning to our seats. Though my traditional Christian beliefs included divine healing, the idea of a healing circle was something I experienced only on occasion.

Spiritual Gathering 2: A different religious assembly I visited opened the service in a manner more in tune with my birth religion. Song books had been placed on our seats, and we began by singing hymns. Often the words differed from the ones I was accustomed to because they had been changed to fit a more open view of life. The rest of the service followed a similar format. Sermon or talk, prayer(s), offering, and announcements. The service ended, however, with psychic messages. The difference this time, was that the psychics were mediums delivering messages from the departed. That was something I had only seen on television, not experienced first-hand.

Feeling a bit uncomfortable, I hoped no one had a message for me. Since no one close to me had died recently, I probably had nothing to fear. In the first religious gathering I described, messages seemed to be given to specific individuals. At this second gathering, the psychics began with a question. "Did somebody lose a mother recently?" or "Who connects with the name Susan or Sherry?"

Spiritual Gathering 3: The next gathering I attended proved to be a balance of my birth-religion and religious gathering number one. The service began with the ringing of a small Tibetan singing bowl followed by a reading from a book of daily devotions.

Once again the sermon was called a talk, but in the case of this assembly it was delivered by a different member of the flock each week, or by a guest speaker. The talks varied greatly due to the different religious backgrounds.

The unspoken rule was to accept what resonated with you and reject anything that didn't. A tolerant, accepting, but also questioning mind was important because the things we believe today might be different from the things we believe in the future. Most weeks, the talk was followed by a group discussion and then a time of silence lasting for about ten minutes. A time to express gratitude came next, followed by individual prayer requests, a summation prayer, and a group prayer for God's protection.

The service concluded with a message given to each person. These messages were short pieces of insight to help or encourage the individual on her or his spiritual journey.

Spiritual Gathering 4: The fourth gathering I encountered had stronger roots in Christianity. Unlike the first three, which rarely used or quoted scripture, the concept of this religious group was to gain a spiritual understanding of the Bible. Instead of taking the Bible literally, they believe in a metaphysical or spiritual interpretation. Members could hold on to their Christian beliefs, yet also go beyond the surface to new realms of spirituality that produces a relationship with The Divine based on personal experience rather than formal traditions. The format of the service was similar to that of Spiritual Gathering 3.

Spiritual Gathering 5: Unity gatherings fall within the boundary of spiritual vs. religious. Though the Unity services—the ones I visited—fall into a more accustomed format, (music, a sermon/talk, and traditional types of prayer), their core beliefs and practices come from a variety of world religions and were my first introduction to new ways of thinking. During their messages/talks I enjoyed the inclusion of advice and insight from other world religions.

One book they seem to pull a lot of wisdom from is *A Course in Miracles*, and the book seems to be almost as important to them as the Bible or the Quran, or any other book that claims Divine inspiration. According to the Unity web site — www.unity.org — their basic teachings may be summed up in five points: 1) God is the source and creator of all. There is no other enduring power. God is good and present everywhere. 2) We are spiritual beings, created in God's image. The spirit of God lives within each person; therefore, all people are inherently good. 3) We create our life experiences through our ways of thinking. 4) There is power in affirmative prayer, which we believe increases our connection to God. 5) Knowledge of these spiritual principles is not enough. We must live them.[4]

Each Sunday the service concluded by joining hands and singing, "Let There Be Peace on Earth," an emotional reminder that peace must begin with individuals and then spread to nations.

Spiritual Gathering 6: The Quaker tradition was built upon the practice of silence—often called "expectant waiting." Though more Christian-based than some of the religious gatherings I've mentioned, it deserves inclusion because of its emphasis on direct communion with The Divine, which is defined by Quakers as Christ and/or God. According to one web site—www.quakerinfo.org – two fundamental beliefs are 1) a belief in the possibility of direct, unmediated communion with the Divine (historically expressed by George Fox in the statement, "Christ is come to teach his people himself"); and 2) a commitment to living lives that outwardly attest to this inward experience.

I am familiar with three types of Quaker services. The un-programmed Quaker meetings entail silence. The first person to enter the sanctuary does so in silence, and all who follow enter in the same attitude of expectant waiting—waiting to hear from The Divine. Meditation and prayer are practiced. In some meetings it is appropriate to speak if and when the individual believes he/she has a word from God to share. Ideally it is given as received, without directing it to an individual and without additional explanation. This appears to be another form of (psychic) message or prophecy.

The Programmed Meetings are led by a minister and follow a traditional format with a message/sermon. The meetings I attended fell into category three and were a hybrid of both, allowing time for a talk, followed by a time of silence.

Like the Unity churches, Quakers are open-minded and service oriented.

Spiritual Gathering 7: The Twelve-Step religious gatherings. Programs such as "Alcoholics Anonymous," "Overeaters Anonymous," "Al-Anon," and others specifically stay away from religious and political entanglements. But in the meetings I have attended I found plenty of spirituality. Their Bible/Torah/Quran is "The Big Book," their commandments are the twelve steps, their ministers, priests, and rabbis are the individual members of the group. The atmosphere exudes love, acceptance, and understanding. Judgments are prohibited.

---

[4] http://content.unity.org/aboutunity/whatWeBelieve/index.html

Their aim is healing. They teach and lead by positive and negative examples. Newcomers are asked to give only their first names and are greeted warmly by everyone present. No dues or fees are collected. Contributions are voluntary. Anonymity is of the utmost importance to all members. Crosstalk is discouraged. The only requirement for attendance is that all members share a common illness: alcohol abuse, drug abuse, overeating, and so forth. Rites of progression are celebrated by all those present.

Within the twelve steps, the phrase "God as we understood Him" appears twice. Another phrase is mentioned in step two, a "Power greater than ourselves." The wording is intentional to make the twelve-step program available to all religious beliefs, and to those with no belief in religion. In step eleven the concept of prayer and meditation is encouraged.

I'm glad the twelve-step program isn't a religion. No outside doctrines have been imposed as to how we should meditate or to whom specifically we should pray. Our religious assemblies could learn from the program. Perhaps we could drop the "church/mosque/synagogue" label and stick with "gatherings" or "programs."

Another characteristic of twelve-step groups I find refreshing is their avoidance of the words "should" and "ought." One member does not instruct another on what he or she should do. Instead they share their personal experiences. They may say, "I had a similar situation, and this is what helped me…"

Nothing's Perfect: In experiencing the different types of spiritual gatherings, I worked hard to keep an open mind. I tried different meetings, returned to the ones I enjoyed the most, and grew accustomed to the new forms. Before long, I embraced them.

Once, when I attended one of my world-religion gatherings, I thought the lady speaker said, "Don't let anyone shit on you." Later that day I asked my wife about it. "No, that's not what she said. She said 'don't let anyone should on you.'" In essence, don't let anyone tell you what you *should* or shouldn't do. Two people may have walked a similar path, but not the exact same one. But, the one who says, "This is what worked for me, maybe it will work for you," gives the listener freedom to decide without pressure or guilt.

One of my favorite phrases is "Take what you like and leave the rest." Perfect. The struggle to be right is avoided, which frees us to be wrong. But right and wrong prove to be elusive. What seemed wrong for one person might be the right thing for another. Often it depends on a person's understanding and frame of reference. There's also the language barrier to consider. Even when we think we speak the same language, we don't. Words have different shades of meaning, and it can often cause misunderstandings. Communication also depends on body language, voice inflection, and emotions.

When we "take what we like and leave the rest," it frees us to come back at a later time to the things we've left. Maybe we left them because we didn't understand what was meant. Later, the recognition comes, and we are grateful. The information has not been pounded into our heads. Instead, the seeds were planted with tenderness, watered with patience, and allowed to grow with rays of love.

Some religious people like to preach. They like to tell us how to live, what to think, how to behave. Yet the world is full of religions and no two are alike. I prefer to have my leaders, guides, teachers, and mentors a little less assertive and a lot more gracious. No two situations are alike. Yes, your child and my child may both be alcoholics or drug addicts, or any number of things, but the way you respond may not be appropriate for me or my child.

At their best, spiritual leaders are messengers. Where they get their message, the spirit in which they receive it, and how they deliver it makes all the difference in how it is received. When the message comes to them, they must first apply it to their own lives before passing it to others. If the messenger speaks of acceptance and love, and then refuses to accept with love and an open mind and heart the validity of different points of view, I question whether he understood his own message.

In twelve-step meetings, the leaders are the individual members of the group, each taking turns leading and sharing. Some who have worked the program longer may have more insight. Those who are new to the program may have more questions and struggles than insights. But as one gives to the other, both heal.

Wouldn't it be nice if spirituality worked in the same way? I receive a message from The Divine, and I apply it to my life first before sharing with others. When I sense it's time to share with another, I carefully word my story to avoid "should-ing" on anyone.

I've tried to keep these descriptions free from bias, but the truth is, I am biased, and, as you may have gathered from reading the foregoing, I do have favorite styles. Because I am most familiar with Christianity, this list does not take into consideration other world religions, and is therefore only a sampling of different practices.

Even though I have been, at times, disappointed in religion, I still hold that "religion" (with a small "r") provides many people a legitimate path to The Divine. Most religions, if not all, started with good intentions, spiritual leadership, and Divinely-appointed purpose. Some may have lost their way—at least to some degree. None is perfect. Wisdom and intuition are needed to find a religious institution that meets the majority of your needs. Remember, the religious gathering that is right for you is the one that works for you. And, over time, that may change.

Before leaving this discussion, however, let's look at some general classifications and some newer forms of worship.

Chapter 3

RELIGIOUS GATHERING LEADERSHIP TYPES

"I love you when you bow in your mosque, kneel in your temple, pray in your church. For you and I are sons of one religion, and it is the spirit."

—Khalil Gibran

The Religious Gathering Tree: Religious gatherings refer to major world religions which include Christianity, Buddhism, Judaism, Hinduism, and more. It also refers to the various factions and fractions that have grown within each type. Christianity, for example, includes Catholics, Protestants, and differing divisions of each. Catholicism includes Byzantine, Traditional, Roman, and differing Eastern and Oriental Catholic churches. Protestant divisions include Lutherans, Anglicans, Calvinists, Congregational, Anabaptists, Baptists, Church of Christ, Holiness churches, and the list goes on.

Denominations split over a variety of issues: What day of the week should be recognized as the Sabbath? Should we use wine or grape juice when we perform the Lord's Supper? Is the ability to speak in tongues required as a sign of holiness?

Other religions experience the same schisms. Buddhism was originally an offshoot of Hinduism. Within Hinduism are at least four branches, Shaivites, Vaishnavas, Smartha, and Shaktism.[5] According to one article, Buddhism can be categorized into three main branches, The Theravada, the Mahayana, and the Vajrayana.[6]

These differences aren't necessarily bad. In fact, many have brought spiritual awakening and renewal. If we view spirituality/religion as a tree, God (Jesus, Buddha, The Divine...) would be the trunk, the various world religions would be the first branches extending upwards, and the different splits within each world belief system would form branches growing upward—a heaven-bound tree of great strength and beauty.

Does spirituality have a place among the branches of our tree? The answer lies in its ability to produce fruit. Does it bring about the qualities of love, compassion, acceptance, and peace? Does it produce better societies? Does it honor all beings? The answer is yes. Spirituality is the life force that courses through the tree.

Other forms of religion have come and gone. They may have held a place among the branches for a time, but failed to produce fruit. Eventually they withered and died, or were pruned away. These include various cults, especially those where the religion was based on an individual claiming to have a direct line with The Divine and demanded unswerving obedience from her or his followers. We've seen the tragedies that result from such blind faith—mass suicides in some cases.

Leader-Based Religious Gathering: There are advantages to traditional religious assemblies. For one, they form a community of friends based on common beliefs, goals,

---

[5] http://www.patheos.com/blogs/whitehindu/2013/01/the-branches-of-hinduism/

[6] http://www.important.ca/three_branches_of_buddhism.html

and expectations. Much like a home, religion promotes friendships that are often as strong as or stronger than family ties. The minister/priest/rabbi takes on a paternal/maternal role. As long as the leader is in tune with the institutional beliefs of their assembly, there is harmony. If the leader steps away from those beliefs, the members of the congregation question the leader's teachings. Is the leader correct, or are the teachings of the religious institution correct? If he fails to satisfy their concerns, he may eventually be removed from leadership. In this way traditional religious groups have a system to prevent falling into a cult.

Once removed, the leader may form a different religious organization. This has proved to be valuable over the centuries. Of course, the new gatherings might also deteriorate into cults. This is the challenge of the New Age and spiritual religious groups, and a word of caution is in order. Be careful of any religious gathering with a strong leader who has all the answers, is inflexible, judgmental, and critical of other religious beliefs. For me, that is a deal breaker.

Perhaps, in my writing, I come across as the leader I just described, one who sits in judgment. That is certainly not my intention. I understand how prone I am to making mistakes. I've made enough mistakes to warrant several lifetimes of bad karma, or several levels of Hell—whatever form of punishment you prefer. My goal is to examine religion with as little prejudice as possible, and if it appears wanting, to point to alternate ways to reach home.

Along with the safety net traditional institutions carry come counterproductive effects. Rigid observance often becomes the norm. Traditions that carried meaning to one generation are not easily dismissed to meet the needs of a changing world. Thinking is restricted. When changes are made, people sometimes rebel.

By declaring to have the way home, and often proclaiming with extreme vigor, this spoken or unspoken belief overrides all other possible roads. There is no wiggle room. The beliefs become so strong that people are willing to kill and die for their path. Holy wars, as ridiculous as that expression is, are fought in the name of religion and even love.

Heaven help us.

The Business Religious Gathering: Religion is big business. Look at the size and beauty of churches, cathedrals, mosques, shrines, temples, and other religious meeting places. Where did the money come from to pay for the elaborate facilities? From believers. Those who stake their lives on the rightness of the religion, a particular leader, and a set of rules invest bucket-loads of money to finance the building and also the hierarchy to maintain the structure and its ministries.

Many religions require members to tithe. Today, tithes are usually considered a tenth of a person's salary, but in past centuries the tithe was often a tenth of a crop, or a tenth of a product.

In Catholicism in the middle ages, the practice of paying for the lessening of sins, known as indulgences, became popular and profitable. The more the people sinned, the more income the Catholic Church received. One cartoon from the sixteenth century depicted a line of sinners waiting to buy indulgences. More rules and regulations equated to more chances to break them, and thus the need to buy more.

Catholicism does not have a monopoly on money manipulation. In 1987 a preacher named Oral Roberts climbed to the top of the prayer tower his ministry had built, and declared he was not coming down until he raised eight million dollars for the support of God's ministry. He claimed God gave him that dollar amount, and if he failed to raise the money, God would take him home.

Television evangelists raise money with emotional appeals (remember Tammy Faye Baker?) to their audiences with promises of God repaying them with better health, greater happiness, and more money. In some religious camps, hard work, sound investment, and saving are replaced by sacrificial giving to the needs of the ministry with the promise that God will abundantly bless the giver with greater wealth and prosperity. When the financial blessing fails to appear, they conveniently point the finger away from their teachings and blame the individual for lack of faith, patience, or both.

The abuse by ministers and their religious gatherings has been documented so often it's a wonder there are those still willing to put their faith in any man of God who promises anything with "a small donation to the ministry." When the religious gathering becomes a business-only venture, preying upon the emotional needs of its members in order to build their personal portfolio, the time comes to withdraw our faith from the person and his/her industry and examine what remains.

Even in the lunacy of those paths that veered off course, there is often something to be salvaged. Yes, the bureaucracy may have been misguided, but within the deception we often find a gem of truth, a simpler path, or a glimmer of hope. Oral Roberts launched his ministry with simple words of hope: "Something good is going to happen to you." Instead of preaching condemnation, hell, and evil, he offered hope. Those deceived by leaders can retain the positive and release the negative. By listening to the voice of God within, they will know when it's time to leave a religious group or a religious leader.

Most religious organizations that become business-based are often also leader-based. No group, however, is exempt. The lure for money, power, and prestige is ever present. With diligence, avoiding the temptations is possible.

A word of caution is in order. I'm not saying using wise business practices to run a religious organization is not recommended. But when the spiritual is missing or faked—

and sometimes it's hard to tell—and all that's left is the business of religion without the soul, it's time to pack up shop.

After reading a very reflective article about Randy Roberts Potts,[7] the gay grandson of Oral Roberts, I believe in his senior years Oral Roberts may have returned to the simple message of his roots. At least, I hope so.

The Social Religious Gathering: Being social is good. There is nothing colder than an unfriendly gathering, especially when a religious meeting becomes exclusive. There is always the danger that when only those who believe, act, and dress according to spoken or unspoken rules gather, they run the risk of limiting their influence to the general public. Sometimes this happens figuratively, and in some situations it happens literally so that no one is permitted without some sort of screening process as is the case in religious cults. "You want to be part of our religious circle? Fine, but first you have to go through _____."

Religious organizations should be spiritual first, social second. With fellowship, openness, acceptance, and nonjudgmental love and forgiveness, religious gatherings flourish. With judgment, criticism, exclusion, and rigidity, religious groups lose spirituality and become social organizations. The wise religious leader battles to bring change, but often with limited results.

Why have many religious gatherings appealed to only one element of society? Why have the buildings been filled with cookie-cutter members who spoke, thought, and looked alike? Religious assemblies fill the role of social groups, and people enjoy socializing with their own kind. Wouldn't it be better to have a mix of races, religions, and ideas working together to discover the spiritual answers sought by all religions throughout time?

Yes, we tend to associate with like-minded people, but the good news is that most assemblies now welcome all types of people. Still, the mix of religions is rarely found.

The Religious Gathering of the Nation: "One nation under God, indivisible, with liberty and justice for all." That phrase is recognized by Americans as part of the pledge of allegiance. It does not spell out what God we are under, be it the Jewish God, the Christian God, or some other God of some other religion. Yet people have argued to have the phrase "under God" removed or preserved.

Our nation was founded upon religious freedom. The fear from some appears to be that Christianity and America will one day mean the same—a theocracy. In other people's mind Christianity and America are synonymous and their fear is that someday

---

[7] http://thislandpress.com/11/18/2012/something-good-is-going-to-happen-to-you/

we will no longer be a Christian nation. I don't want to weigh in on the rightness of removing or retaining the phrase. Smarter minds than mine can sort through that question.

I also understand that America leads the way in religious tolerance, and I believe it always will. I don't want to criticize but to encourage. Let's go even further than we have in the past. Let's lead the way by creating assemblies that embrace the faiths of all nations.

I don't believe we will ever become a one-religion nation. The nation of Israel has a national religion, and I see no getting around it—at least not in the near future. They have also faced great tribulation throughout their history—hated by other nations, constant wars and fighting—they face problems that other nations have avoided. I'm not saying they are wrong or right. I accept their right to believe as they do. I don't have to agree with them. Since I grew up in a Christian home and studied the Bible, I respect the Old Testament and its wisdom. I disagree with them, however, when they believe—like other religions—they have a monopoly on The Divine.

The Hospital Religious Gathering: I recall an incident that happened years ago. An elderly man sat unattended in a wheelchair on an elevator. People got on, people got off. No one paid particular notice. He rode up and down all day until he expired. His death wasn't discovered until late evening.

Ironically, the elevator he rode to his death was located inside a hospital. The place he had gone for help and health became the place that delivered neither.

I try to avoid religious groups that operate in the same way. As people go through the ups and downs of life, they often seek help and health from religious organizations. Accidents happen, of course, but when religious gatherings fail to notice those who are about to spiritually expire, we wonder what went wrong. I recall an old expression about the church being the only organization that buries its wounded.

Most religious organizations incorporate some form of healing in their beliefs. The range includes healing prayers, laying on of hands, revival-style healing where people are "slain in the Spirit," emotional healing, spiritual healing sometimes conducted through confession or altar calls, and newer forms of healing such as acupuncture, reiki, psychic medical diagnosis, and more. One of the most dramatic forms of healing is the exorcism.

When considering a religious organization, the form of healing a group subscribes to determines, at least in part, the comfort zone of its audience. I have never been comfortable with flamboyant healers. Others have. I'm not completely comfortable with some of the newer forms, either. In fact, I am most comfortable with perhaps the mildest form of healing: spiritual healing.

Specifically, I believe that forgiveness can heal individuals and the world of the majority of the afflictions that plague us. Others are perfectly comfortable with different forms of healing, and perhaps one day I will be, too. The issue here is not right or wrong. It's simply what a person resonates with.

We don't want to get stuck on an elevator going nowhere. But, at the same time, stretching our comfort zone can lead to experiences that enrich our lives.

When I think about healing, I'm drawn to the story of Dumbo, the Disney cartoon character, and his oversized ears. So large, in fact were his ears, that they caused mishap and misery. His only friend, Timothy Q. Mouse, tried to cheer him by taking him to see his mother. On the return home, they drink from a water bucket that was accidentally laced with champagne. The next morning the pair find themselves in a tree, uncertain how they got there. Timothy is convinced Dumbo (the baby elephant) flew them there using his oversized ears.

Timothy Mouse convinces Dumbo he can fly by the use of a magical feather. If he holds onto the feather, he has the ability to soar. At the end of the story, Dumbo loses the feather, but Timothy convinces him there was never anything magical about the feather, and that he still has the ability to fly.

Is religious healing no more than a magical feather? For that matter, is physical healing with doctors and hospitals also not based in part on the belief of the patient that modern medicine—pills, surgery, physical therapy—will cure them? Another magical feather?

I don't know. But, if it works, what difference does it make? Hold onto the feather as long as you need. If it stops working, grab something else. I've been fortunate in that I've lived a healthy physical life. But, like others, I needed healing from religious pain and disease. I've grasped at feathers, held on, and discovered the ability to soar above religion. But, I've also made it on my own without the props, discovering that the ability to soar was with me all the time.

We know the way home. We just have to trust our Inner Guide.

The Flock-Based Religious Gathering: Earlier we considered the twelve-step spiritual meeting, referring to programs such as Alcoholics Anonymous. They meet wherever they can find inexpensive rent. They may have one or two individuals who organize the initial meeting, but it isn't long before the meetings are overseen by the attendees themselves. General guidelines are used instead of commandments or rules. The one exception might be the adherent to complete anonymity. Their meetings survive solely on the participation of those who attend. No one is required to speak, but all are welcome to share.

Without participation the meetings would die. Amazing. No preacher. No priests. Yet the people come, share, heal, love, socialize, and receive nearly everything you would want from a spiritual gathering.

I'm not opposed to religion. In fact, one of my goals is for people to appreciate what religious faith has to offer in spite of whatever hurts, in the name of religion, may have been committed against them. Perhaps a new twelve-step group, "Religious Recovery," could be formed to help those who have been injured and have turned away from their birth religions.

Lately, I seem to have come across a number of agnostics. Good. Better to have someone who is uncertain than one who claims to have all the answers and wants to pound them into me. The agnostics I've met are honest. When I am most vulnerable, I admit—at least to myself—there is no way to know for certain if there is a Higher Power. I have not met The Divine face-to-face. I have not literally heard His/Her voice. Personal experiences have led me to believe in a Divine Other, but to be able to show incontrovertible proof is not possible.

I also find hope in knowing that the pursuit of The Divine is found in all nations. So, I learn from those who are seeking, just like I am. That's why I like the idea of a flock-based assembly where every man, woman, and child is a priest, where all share, and where criticism is discouraged, love is exchanged, hope happens, and all are welcome.

For some, the twelve-step meeting appears to be transitional. People come for a time, heal, and move on. No problem. Others who attend, heal, fall in love with the program, and choose to stay to help. It doesn't matter. Whenever people are involved, difficulties arise. But in spite of the people, the twelve-step programs succeed.

There *is* a place for the twelve-step spiritual gathering—a place for simple, back-to-the-basics caring for one another's needs through love and through listening and offering simple advice in a take-what-you-like-and-leave-the-rest formula.

An unspoken premise in twelve-step meetings is that people know intuitively what advice to take and what to leave. This releases the person sharing from owning another's healing. My situation may be similar to yours, but it can't be exactly the same. What works for me may not work for you. That's okay. It's not my job to fix anyone except myself. Besides, someone else may benefit from my sharing, and often the one who benefits the most is the individual who shares.

Chapter 4
RELIGIOUS GATHERINGS AT HOME

"But when you pray, go into your room, close the door..."
—Jesus[8]

---

[8] Matthew 6:6 (NIV)

Solitary Services: For a number of years I attended a private church I call "Bedside Baptist: Church of the Inner Spring." I've never been a Baptist; I just like the alliteration. Other religious gatherings exist, and perhaps you have attended one of these private meetings: "Mattress Methodist," "Closet Calvinist," "Lazy-Boy Lutheran," or "Couch Potato Catholic – the names abound, and these personal religious gatherings aren't all Christian. There are the "Home Hindu," the "Brookside Buddha," the "Isolated Islam," and the "Solitary Shaman."

Is it possible to hold private religious gathering services where only one attends?

Religion would argue no. A religious meeting entails the coming together of community for worship, instruction, and fellowship or community.

Spirituality says yes, it is possible. For the spiritual person a religious gathering isn't about an external building but an internal relationship. Services have their place, but nothing substitutes for seeking The Divine within. Jesus said "the kingdom of God is within you."[9] He never raised money to build a sanctuary, never hired a publicist, and he never sought the limelight.

He spoke to those who would listen. He healed those who came to him. Quite often he pulled away from the crowd and sought sanctuary in solitude—in meditation and prayer. He battled temptation in the wilderness—alone. Nature was his synagogue, the earth his altar, and the sky the open dome of his cathedral.

I worship at my own private religious gathering, usually in the early morning hours when I'm supposed to be sleeping. In recent years these services have become more meaningful. But there was a time when my private communion with The Divine paled in comparison to a traditional gathering. At least in some respects. I've always enjoyed spiritual music—songs that speak of The Divine. I've had different favorites, but the threads that run through them are emotional, inspirational, and insightful. In my private religious gatherings the music was, for the most part, absent.

There were no sermons in my private meetings. No lectures, no one instructing me on right and wrong, no one collecting money, and no weekly announcements. Just me, the bed sheets, and the ceiling.

Disillusioned: This was the period when religion had disillusioned me. Shortly before my marriage came to an end, I left the church of my childhood where I had served as a staff minister for three years. After trying a variety of religious institutions and deciding on a religious group with a more liberal theology and music program, I found myself

---

[9] Luke 17:21

disappointed that the scope of their acceptance was more limited than I had hoped—and needed.

That's when I discovered the Prostrate Presbyterian Pew, otherwise known as my bed. Many people can relate to my experience and have similar stories to share of their own disappointments with religious organizations. Morning quiet times were spent in prayer, which consisted in reciting a list of names of people I prayed for. No Bible reading, little or no meditation, and little or no spiritual growth.

To a close friend I jokingly confided I had become a heathen. During that desert time, my faith in religion bottomed out. Nevertheless, I was still spiritual. Still held to the simple idea that something greater than myself was in charge of the universe. But I questioned religion and authority.

Due to my divorce, I was no longer accepted as a minister in my former denomination. I was not good enough. I understood and acknowledged their decision, but I could not accept their judgmental attitudes. It's one thing to be told you *did* wrong, quite another to be told you *are* wrong.

New Light: I found meaning in my private meetings only after I found my way back to a more traditional religious gathering, which is often the case. My experience caused me to doubt many of my beliefs. When I found a religious group that accepted those doubts, in fact often encouraged me to think for myself, I found new light and new hope.

Since then, my morning quiet times have become a rich experience. I often wake between the hours of four and six. Once my eyes focus I begin reading. Now, I rarely read from the Bible. Years of reading the Bible through from beginning to end, Bible memorization, and Bible stories gave me a wealth of knowledge to draw upon. What I lacked was a broader base of understanding. That's when my attention was draw to Oprah, Wayne Dyer and a new way of understanding.

I was unfamiliar with the New Age movement. What was all the hoopla? Was there anything to it? My prior church experience dismissed New Age thought. Except for Wayne Dyer, I wasn't familiar with New Age authors. The only title that came to mine was a book written in the 1980s by Shirley MacLaine. When she came out with her book, *Out on a Limb*, a part of the Christian community abhorred her teachings and labeled them as heresy. In fact, F. LeGard Smith authored a book titled *Out on a Broken Limb*.

But MacLaine's book had been written in the 1980s, and I wanted to discover what was currently popular. There was plenty of material available, and before long I was reading books that stretched my beliefs and my credulity. Some authors claimed their works were channeled from sources outside the five senses. Their claim went beyond inspiration or the writer's muse to the realm of spirits, guides, and in some cases, Divine authority.

How could I accept these works as being from God? But, don't religions ask for the same act of faith—that God spoke directly to man thousands of years ago? To believe God could and did speak to men in the past, but no longer does so in the present, seems a greater stretch of credulity.

Arguments arise claiming if God were to speak today, then those words must be measured against the Bible, as if that was God's final word to our planet. Note that I am, for the moment, speaking from a Christian background, ignoring the other world religions that believe they have an exclusive claim on God and His word. But what applies to one, applies to the others. What seems to be overlooked by most Christians is the new religious truth that was brought to the world through John the Baptist, Jesus, and the apostles.

At some point it seems the age of revelation was closed. Yet, it seems as if Martin Luther said, taught, and demonstrated that it was not. Others followed who also claimed in deed if not by their words that the Divine Other was still speaking. (Today, the concept that divine revelation is closed seems to be a passé belief.)

The teachings of Jesus ruffled a lot of feathers in the spiritual community of his day. In fact, at one point they asked if Jesus wasn't the son of Joseph, and if so, how could he claim to be from heaven and make such wild statements. In one passage of Scripture, Jesus took the law and added to it. He understood the deeper, spiritual meaning behind the law and tried to explain it to his listeners. Not only should you not kill, but to be angry with a brother or sister is a mistake. Why? Because murder begins with anger, so to harbor anger is to withhold love, and love was the fulfilling of the law.

If we believe Jesus brought in new spiritual truth, or if we believe Moses delivered new words from God, then is it not reasonable to believe that The Divine still communicates today, or has The Divine run out of things to say?

Even with the new truth that Jesus, Moses, Mohammed, and Buddha brought into the world, no one seems to agree about what that truth is and how to apply it. Take the Christian community for example. Some faiths believe in immersion as the only form of baptism. Some don't. Some believe in foot washings. Others don't. Some speak in tongues. Who is right? Who is wrong?

Shouldn't the foundation of faith begin with love and proceed with forgiveness toward all beings—including ourselves—and also be based on acceptance and gratitude?

I explored other writers, other religions, and other thought systems. For years I'd heard about *A Course in Miracles*, so I delved into it. By recommendation or by happenstance, I discovered the writings of other spiritual teachers. Some teachers proved meaningful and helpful, others not so much. After reading books that taught ways to draw closer to

The Divine, I opened my mind to meditation and prayer, usually focused more on the former. I was burned out from years of praying for people and found myself developing a mindset of "God knows what I need before I ask. I may not know what it is I need, so I'll ask The Divine to show me."

Like many people, I struggled with meditation. Years ago I'd read Richard Foster's book, *Celebration of Discipline*, an excellent guide to the traditional spiritual disciplines, including meditation, but I'd forgotten about that book and its methods. Upon the recommendation of a friend, I attended a local Zen Center to discover the secrets of the religions of the East.

There were no secrets. Simply concentrate on the breath in an effort to still the mad monkey mind. The challenge proved to be nearly impossible. After opening with a few chants, we stayed in silence for eighty minutes. After the session, I chatted with one of the leaders.

"I can't empty my mind," I confessed.

"Who said you're supposed to?"

"I thought that was the idea?"

"If you empty you're mind, think nothing, you'll be dead."

I'd never considered that idea, but he was right.

"The idea is to still the mind, focus the mind. Quiet the raging thoughts."

I nodded, feeling I could do that.

"Try noticing your thoughts as if you're an observer. You hear a horn blast from a car outside. Try not to react. Don't get frustrated because you're no longer focused on your breath. In your mind, say to yourself, 'I hear a car horn. Huh.' Then immediately return to the breath."

The power of meditation comes from quieting the mind until the spirit calms allowing us to see beyond our everyday concerns in order to see the larger picture. Meditation allows for contemplation which powerfully transforms our problem-solving abilities. When I'm speaking, writing, or teaching, I use meditation/contemplation to prepare.

Meditation allows me—allows each of us—to connect to our intuition and Higher Power. We can hear the divine whispers. Chaos created by the anxious mind tries to overpower the voice of The Divine, but that Voice is still there—just more difficult to hear. In addition, the ego brings to mind a thousand things that need to be done, should be done, ought to be done; situations that could-have/would-have/should-have been different if only this or that had been done instead. But in meditation we strive to silence the chaos, matters of past and future, the ego, and all other interruptions to the present moment.

A good way to begin is to concentrate on the breath. If you take a glass with sediment in the bottom and swirl it, the water becomes murky. If you stop swirling and allow the debris to settle, the water clears and vision opens.

Meditation/contemplation works the same way. By allowing the muck to settle, we can examine a situation more clearly, and by listening for the Divine Voice we gain understanding and direction. All of this can be accomplished in the privacy of your home.

Jesus said when we pray we should go into our room and shut the door. That's not to say that we can't experience Divine Presence in nature, or at religious institutions, or in a million other places and situations; but when we want one-on-one time to seek answers or to draw closer, alone-time brings the results we seek.

A Missed Appointment: A number of years ago, before the modern ubiquity of cell phones, I scheduled a meeting with a friend at a local restaurant. I arrived early and asked if anyone had arrived alone looking for me. To their knowledge, no one had, but I was invited to look around.

Satisfied that I had arrived first, I took my seat. I waited a short while and then decided to use the restroom. When I returned my table was still empty. I decided my friend had forgotten or something had come up. I used the payphone and called. Maybe I had written down the wrong date. I got the answering machine.

I left a message, returned to my seat, waited awhile longer, ate and left. At home I discovered a message on my answering machine.

"Wayne," the voice of my friend said, "I was there. I got there a few minutes after the hour and looked for you."

"How could that be?" I wondered. But, it happened. We were in the same restaurant at the same time, evidently in different areas, and we failed to connect.

There are times in prayer/meditation when I feel the same way. I work to quiet my mind and connect with The Divine. Yet the noise and activity of my mind obstruct my connection with The Divine with me—within me—speaking softly, waiting for me to settle into a place where I can hear His Voice, feel Her Presence, and know.

When I find myself struggling with quiet time, my restaurant experience reminds me to be still and know. Just as my friend had been present in the restaurant, yet we failed to connect, The Divine is always present and a little patience and attentive listening can help make the connection. A simple sentence from *A Course in Miracles* says it in a slightly different way:

"Into Your Presence, would I enter now."

That simple phrase allows me to make a mental and sometimes emotional shift. When I lie in bed in the morning preparing for bedside worship, I say the words in my head and in my heart, with just a slight variation: "Into Your Presence I would enter now." I do not define who or what that presence is in religious terms, but it is my Higher Power.

That which was, is, and shall always be. That which created me, sustains me, loves me, and abides in me—no matter what.

Is it possible to have a religious gathering of one? Yes, especially for those with multiple personalities.

I wrote that last sentence in jest. But truth is, we all have multiple personalities. All things spiritual begin—and ultimately end—with "we."

Chapter 5
LIGHT GUIDES THE WAY

"Darkness cannot drive out darkness:
only light can do that."
> — **Martin Luther King, Jr.**

Reverend King's quest was to drive out the darkness of racial prejudice. The time has come for the world to throw off religious prejudice.

In an orchestra or band every member has an instrument to play, a contribution to make. As a youth, I played the trumpet for a while. I sat in the orchestra with other trumpet players. The best trumpet player was given the position of first chair and made section leader.

I loved the sound of the trumpet—loud, commanding, piercing, yet soft and delicate when the music demanded. I liked knowing that the trumpet parts were prominent in many scores—that I would have a share in carrying the melody. I knew there were more instruments in the orchestra, of course, but I liked the trumpet section and had a world of my own with like-minded trumpet players.

There was, of course, only one conductor. How silly it would have been to have two or more conductors vying for leadership. One conductor, several section leaders, many musicians, all coming together in beautiful harmony, each making her or his own special contribution.

What would happen if a section decided that it was more important than the others? That its way of making music was the only right way? What would happen if that section criticized the other sections and accused them of doing it wrong, claiming that if they didn't get on board, they would be thrown out of the orchestra and never be seen or heard from again, condemned to orchestra hell playing with the banjos and accordions?

One conductor—many sections. All music leads to the final glorious symphony.

One God—many religions, but all roads lead home.

Each instrument plays off its own music sheet. The oboes have a different sheet of music than the violins, and the percussion section has an entirely different music sheet. But combined and coordinated under the direction of the skilled conductor, they produce a beautiful sound.

Mahatma Gandhi wrote: "Each one prays to God according to his own light." Or, to follow the analogy further, each musician—no matter the instrument—seeks guidance from the same conductor. The wisdom given may be specific to that particular instrument, musician, or passage of music, but that doesn't make it right for all instruments, all musicians, or for all passages of music.

To insist that because I have been given specific instructions from the Conductor, everyone else must accept my light as their own, is short-sighted. The Conductor may tell me to play loud and quick, and instruct the violins to play one long note—softly. At the same time, He may instruct the oboes to be still. Listen, and watch for His cue before playing again.

Though not everyone travels the same highway, all roads eventually lead home. We follow the Light (intuition, guidance, spiritual instruction and other practices that resonate with us) and allow others to do the same.

Living in the Light of religious freedom begins with tolerating, moves to accepting, and eventually ends with creating community. We don't all have to be trumpet players or violinists or drummers. We accept the varying sections of the orchestra without prejudice.

The Light That Leads Us Can Also Frighten Us: "Our deepest fear is not that we are inadequate. Our deepest fear is that we are powerful beyond measure. It is our Light, not our Darkness, that most frightens us" –Marianne Williamson.

Again we stumble upon the problem of right versus wrong. If you are completely right, I must be completely wrong. If the proponents of Christianity who claim theirs is the only way are right, then those who disagree must be wrong and destined for hell. The same must be said of Islam and all other religions that claim exclusivity.

If the Light tells us all religions have worth, then our form of religion—if it claims to be the only path—has lied, and that should concern us and make us question our rigidity. Millions of people are Christians. Then again, millions of people are Muslims, Hindus, Buddhists, Jews, or atheists. Each group believes it is right.

Each group claims to have its own Light. The sun shines the same on all nations of the world. We may respond differently depending on our traditions, but the Light doesn't change. The same is true of religion—at least it should be. If it does hold a measure of the Light, it brightens our path and leads our way back to the Source. But, that doesn't mean the Light of another path doesn't produce the same illumination to guide its adherents.

At its best, religion leads us home. But, when religion blocks the Light, or tells us the Light within us is not the real Light, we have problems. Spirituality steps forward to remind us we are all children of Divine Power, an Eternal Father-Mother Being, and that the Light within each child comes from the highest Source.

We all want assurance on our journey—want someone, or perhaps better still, some group of people, who know where they're going and who claim to have a GPS to get there. The problem is, many people have GPSes, and not all are made by the same company. If my GPS has a map of Canada, and your GPS has a map of Puerto Rico, how can they get us to the same destination?

There is a built-in Guidance system within us that will, if we follow the Light, enable us to find our way. Why then are we afraid of the Light? We believe there is safety in numbers, so we follow the crowd. At times, and for many, the crowd leads us in the right direction. At other times, the crowd is wrong, and only by listening to the Light within are we able to take the proper turn in the road. That's not to say the crowd may not at some point hear the gentle Voice proclaim "Recalculating."

The Light within might frighten us when it leads us on an overgrown, lonely path. But follow we must. Fears may overwhelm us, and we may sense we've lost the Light when we stumble through the briars, but the secluded path has its purpose.

Though following the Light, Martin Luther, leader of the Reformation, discovered such a lonely path when he delivered his "The Ninety-Five Theses" in a letter he wrote to his bishop. It was meant only as a discourse on his belief that it was improper to sell indulgences—improper to believe that man's soul could be saved from hell through the purchase of indulgences.

Martin Luther obeyed the Light, Pope Leo X excommunicated him from the Catholic Church, and the Roman Emperor Charles V condemned him as a criminal. Still, he refused to deny the Light, and thus sparked a spiritual reformation, new religious beliefs, and eventual changes in Catholicism.

Mohandas Karamchand Gandhi, (commonly known as Mahatma Gandhi), also followed the Light and faced difficult roads. In South Africa he fought for civil rights both for Muslims and Hindus. He created the strategy of non-violent civil disobedience in order to affect change by speaking to the Light of The Divine in his opponents. After moving to India, he led—in the name of what was right—campaigns for lower taxes, the rights of Muslims, and women's rights. And he led a nationwide campaign for Indian independence from British rule.

The British imprisoned Gandhi on several occasions, yet he continued to follow his Light and reached out to all kinds of people and all religious groups.

In the end, each of us must decide to hide from the Light or welcome it. If we believe Light comes through only one leader or one religious organization, we cut ourselves off from any enlightenment (in-Light-en-ment) we could have achieved. Failure to learn from other paths only brings spiritual darkness.

When I've opened myself to Light from another source, I've found myself challenged and overwhelmed. But eventually, my spiritual eyes adjust and new Light shines through. This happens not only for me, but for all of us if we choose to seek new sources of Light.

The Unknown Road

"A good traveler has no fixed plans, and is not intent on arriving."
—Lao Tzu

Religions claim to know the final destination but none seem to agree on where or what it is. Christianity calls home "heaven" and describes it as a city with twelve gates, streets of gold, a high throne called The Mercy Seat where God sits with Jesus on his right hand. Other accounts describe angels surrounding the throne, constantly proclaiming "Holy,

Holy, Holy." Other angels proclaim and bless the name of God without ending. Jesus, however, proclaimed that the kingdom of God was within us.

Islam also calls "heaven" home and describes it as having rivers of water, rivers of milk, rivers of wine, and rivers of honey. Believers are rewarded for their patience with garments of silk.[10] Temperatures will be moderate, fruit abundant, and vessels of silver and cups of crystal will be given to those who achieve paradise.

Buddhists do not believe in an eternal heaven or, for that matter, an eternal hell. Hell is temporary and anyone can work their way out of it. They believe there are heavens and hells not only beyond this world but also within the world around us and within us. For the Buddhist, there is nothing worse than the hell of anger, lust, greed, or ignorance.

Heaven is also temporary and is the dwelling place where one goes when he has done good deeds. While in heaven, one experiences sensual pleasures. The number of heavens in Buddhism varies according to the different sects.

Just from examining three different religions, we find that the final destination of man is described differently. If a Muslim died and went to Christian heaven, would he recognize it, or would he conclude he had not lived a good enough life and landed in hell? The same could be said of a Christian who died and woke up in a state called Nirvana. Would he be so dogmatic in his beliefs as to conclude he had somehow ended up in hell—with or without the eternal fire?

If it cannot be determined which heaven is right, then why not sit back and enjoy the ride. What would happen if our travels led us to no particular destination? What would we conclude then?

Perhaps the journey is the destination. This opens our mind to the possibility that all descriptions of our final destination—home—might be right, and that all might be wrong. Each may have a measure of truth, but all may fall short of the total picture. We return to the example of the blind men and the elephant—all had a portion of the truth, but only through their collective "sight" could the best image of the elephant come together.

As an ancient Chinese proverb says, "Don't curse the darkness. Light a candle." Each candle we light illuminates the darkness and gives us better vision. We may not know where the soul goes after death, or what that place looks like, but the collective belief of all religions gives us hope for a different and better existence beyond this life.

Should we be discouraged if we do not have a clear picture of the final destination? We want to know there's a pot of gold at the end of the rainbow. We love our happy

---

[10] The Qur'an 76: 12-21

endings—it gives us something to live for, hope for, and dream of.

But what if the end we seek is far greater than we could ever imagine? What if each religion can only describe a small portion of what is to come? And what if, heaven forbid, the place we seek is not so much a physical location, but a reuniting, a remembering, and a state of heart that has always been within our grasp? What if that final destination is simply a return to the place from which we started, and is indeed, within the heart, spirit, and soul of every man, woman, and child?

Reward and punishment have served a purpose in religion. Fear of punishment and the hope of reward have shaped conduct and supplied reasons to stay true to the faith. But, what is the mission of religious belief? Is it merely to shape character, or is it to point the way back to The Divine? Is shaping character and the pursuit of a moral standard the only way to gain entrance to our eternal home?

Can we have a world free of the proverbial divine carrot stick and red, pitchfork-carrying villain? If we dispense with reward and punishment and set as our goal something simpler, will we fall into disbelief, or will we discover purpose and meaning inherent within the individual?

I love the descriptions of heaven that religions offer. I hope in some way we all experience a measure of heaven, nirvana, paradise, bliss, whatever you choose to call it. But, the best way to look forward to the afterlife is to fully experience this present life. To find peace, love, acceptance of our fellow man, our nations, and ourselves. To find meaning and purpose for what we set our hands to do. To live each moment as a gift.

We can have heaven on earth if we lay aside our differences and concentrate on our similarities. There's nothing wrong with having goals as long as they don't interfere with living life. And, if I find this life meaningless and disappointing, will I find the afterlife any different? But, if I search for and find happiness in this life, won't that happiness reflect in the life to come, creating a richer and fuller experience?

Chapter 6
FORGIVENESS: PATH TO PEACE

"Peace comes from within. Do not seek it without."
—Buddha

"Blessed are the peacemakers, for they will be called children of God."
—Jesus[11]

---

[11] Matthew 5:9

Tolerance: Peace is as elusive as the rainbow. Just when you think you've almost caught it, the image moves further away or vanishes completely. It's the same for personal peace, relational peace, national peace, or world peace.

The religions of the world could lead the way, but unfortunately history has shown a different outcome. The first step is tolerance. As President Barack Obama said, "America and Islam are not exclusive and need not be in competition. Instead, they overlap, and share common principles of justice and progress, tolerance and the dignity of all human beings."

That particular quote may be offensive to some. Intolerance towards the nation of Islam is prevalent in American society. But tolerance works best when it begins with individuals—no matter what nationality they are. When the people demand tolerance of other nations, of other governments, and of other political or religious belief systems, then the leaders follow. The time for violence and war is at an end, and the time to recognize our brothers and sisters has arrived.

Acceptance: Following closely on the heels of tolerance is acceptance. Tolerance is more of a gritting-the-teeth consent, but acceptance goes a step further. Tolerance stomachs only so much, but acceptance lays aside differences and moves a step closer to unity. Tolerance has the undertone of resignation, whereas acceptance bespeaks positive change.

William James wrote, "Acceptance of what has happened is the first step to overcoming the consequences of any misfortune." To go further, acceptance of what needs to happen is also a step forward. The world has been through countless wars and still we find reasons to hate. Reasons to kill our brothers and sisters—all too often in the name of religion.

In recent decades the call to peace and to lay down our arms has grown strong. Tolerating different opinions and accepting others' right to live, govern, and worship as they please moves us closer to peace.

Forgiveness: Tolerance and acceptance coupled with forgiveness provide the best formula for permanent change. If we look at the history of racial prejudice we see this pattern emerges—not always in a specific order, but each element of the process is included. Forgiveness feels forced when we can't stand to be in the same room with another person based solely on their skin color. Acceptance moves us closer to forgiveness. But is it possible to forgive first, and then allow the other feelings to catch up?

Forgiveness is a decision and an emotion. We can choose to forgive even when we don't feel like it. In fact, we must often begin with the decision in order to open the door to communication and understanding.

Numerous illustrations of the effect of forgiveness abound, but the Amish school shooting in Bart Township, Pennsylvania on October 2, 2006 demonstrates how a community can overcome a heinous act without falling into hatred, condemnation, and a demand for retribution.

On that fall Monday, Charles Roberts IV entered an Amish schoolroom carrying a Springfield XD 9mm handgun and took ten girls, aged 6-13, hostage. He eventually wounded five and killed the other five before taking his own life. The details are gruesome, but the response of the community went beyond tolerance and acceptance to forgiveness.

I'm certain the family members and friends of the dead and wounded felt anger, rage, and even hatred. But they chose to respond with forgiveness. A grandfather of one of the murdered girls advised younger relatives not to hate the killer. "We must not think evil of this man," he said.

Another father spoke of the killer's own mother and father, about the fact that Charles Roberts also had a soul—and that he now stood before a just God. There were more than ten victims that day. Charles Roberts IV and his family were also victims. Charles Roberts was a victim of a twisted, mentally unbalanced mind, and his parents lost their son. His death made national news, and in the eyes of the world, Charles Roberts was a monster.

Still, the community responded with loving forgiveness. An Amish neighbor comforted the Roberts family for hours, and others followed that example with visits and words of comfort and forgiveness.

Some have criticized the reaction of the Amish. How could they forgive a gunman who had shown no remorse for what he had done? How could they move from such a devastating tragedy and seem to bypass tolerance, acceptance, denial, rage, and bitterness?

Letting go of grudges is a deeply rooted value for the Amish. A grudge harms the one who holds it more than the pain of the initial injustice. Forgiveness is as much for the one who gives as it is for the one who receives. Perhaps more so.

When we refuse to forgive, we are the ones who lose. We lose our peace. We lose sight of the deeper issues of life. We lose our ability to love without conditions. When we forgive, we receive. We receive peace. We trust in a higher purpose. And we enlarge our capacity to love—and to be loved.

The ability of the Amish community to forgive is no secret. They simply practice it in their daily lives, and when tragedy strikes, the investment of forgiveness—contributed to over years of daily releasing small grudges—pays big dividends.

Forgiveness does not lessen the tragedy, but it provides a way to walk through it. Forgiveness does not set the guilty free from punishment, but it gives the victims freedom from further pain and suffering.

Justice or Mercy? I came across this question a few years ago: "What is more important, justice or mercy?" The question was pulled randomly from a game called "Table Topics." I had seconds to formulate an answer. As quickly as possible, I considered the ramifications of each answer. With time ticking away, I chose mercy. I haven't regretted that choice.

Justice goes back to "an eye for an eye." Mercy goes forward to "Love your enemies." The problem with justice is that it never satisfies. How do you give justice to the Amish families whose children were wounded or murdered? Five lives were taken. According to "an eye for an eye," doesn't justice call for five lives to be taken in return? Charles Roberts IV took his own life, thus robbing the families of "the sweet taste of revenge," which, in reality, is not sweet at all. What of the other four lives owed in revenge? His mother and father? Siblings, if any? And if he had no siblings, then grandparents, children, friends? Where does it end?

That's the problem: it doesn't end with an eye for an eye. We want to make sure the punishment is greater. The pain inflicted on the guilty must be worse than what the victims suffered. Death is not enough because they don't have to live in misery over what they did.

Unfortunately, as wars have demonstrated, revenge rarely ends quickly or without tremendous loss. We can break the cycle and bring peace through mercy and forgiveness, and by following the appeal to "love your enemies" and to "do good to those who hurt you." This is religion and spirituality at its highest. This is the call to lay down our religious and political arms and live in peace.

Embrace: Only after forgiveness can the last two steps emerge. We're not just talking about a physical embrace. That can be given without emotion or sincerity, although even a bad embrace can be better than none, because it can open the heart. The simple act of touch has power for change.

The embrace we speak of is one of mental assent, of friendship, and at least of a hint of a love relationship between two people, two differing beliefs, or two nations. Albert Einstein wrote: "Our task must be to free ourselves from this prison by widening our circle of compassion to embrace all living creatures and the whole of nature in its beauty."

We imprison ourselves when we refuse to embrace another. When pride, prejudice, problems, petty jealousies, or clouded vision prevents us from seeing our enemies are no better or worse—in fact no different than we are, then we imprison ourselves. Tolerance, acceptance, and forgiveness are the tools that chip away at the walls, allowing us to widen our circle of compassion, and thus giving us the freedom to embrace every living person as created in the image of The Divine.

We exclude no one. No matter who they are or what they have done, we cherish all humanity. We determine to stop judging, start accepting, and open ourselves to other ways of living. Once we have embraced them mentally, we are able to embrace our neighbors with open arms. The definition of embrace includes open arms, for how can we embrace physically with closed arms? How can we embrace mentally with closed minds?

Picture a yogi sitting cross-legged with arms extended wide to the left and right. An open-arm invitation for The Divine to fill him with love and guidance, but also an open-arm invitation to embrace the world by extending the love and guidance he receives to every living being.

Picture Jesus with arms extended to the world, inviting all to come to him. We can also picture the same image for Buddha, and for all who have known an intimate connection with The Divine. The ability to embrace our enemies, family, and friends is a test of spiritual authenticity.

Love: The culmination of the first four steps is love. The culmination of religion and spirituality is love—or it should be. In the first chapter we considered the golden rule and how it appears in one form or another in most of the world's religions. In fact, in several instances there is the inclusion of an expression that gives it prime importance.[12]

Islam: The religion of Islam stresses this so emphatically that adherence to it determines true belief. "*No one of you is a believer* until he desires for his brother that which he desires for himself." —Sunnah

Hinduism: Religious responsibility is fulfilled through the golden rule in Hinduism. "*This is the sum of duty;* do naught onto others what you would not have them do unto you."[13]

Judaism: The Law is of utmost importance in Judaism which makes this statement all the more compelling. "What is hateful to you, do not do to your fellowman. *This is the entire Law; all the rest is commentary.*"[14]

Christianity: Jesus gave the golden rule second place only to the command to Love

---

[12] Italics were added to some of these quotes for emphasis.

[13] Mahabharata 5,1517

[14] Talmud, Shabbat 3id

God with all your heart. Then he emphasized its importance when he added, "*There is no commandment greater than these.*"[15]

Religions, governments, and societies as we know them could fade away if everyone practiced the simple mandate to do unto others as you would want them to do to you. Do you want them to love you? Then you must love them. Do you want them to respect you? Respect them. Do you want them to hear you, accept you, and acknowledge your worth? Do the same to them.

We are not perfect. Even in our attempts to love we make mistakes. The path to peace is not easy. That's why we have been given the ability to tolerate, accept, forgive, embrace, and love. Each opportunity to hate presents us the chance to practice the path to peace. Each hurt, each grudge, each unkind word or deed provides an occasion for growth. One incident at a time, we build up Divine characteristics based on simply doing unto others what we would want done to us.

---

[15] Mark 12: 28-31

Chapter 7
RELIGIOUS ADDICTION

*"Every form of addiction is bad,
no matter whether the narcotic be
alcohol or morphine or idealism."*

–Carl Jung

I would suggest religion and spirituality fall under Jung's category of idealism. Religion and spirituality provide a different form of "high." A safer high than narcotics, alcohol, or morphine perhaps, but still a different level of consciousness.

I've heard people say, "I used to be addicted to drugs and alcohol. Now I'm addicted to Jesus" (or Buddha, or Krishna, or Mohammed…).

Nothing wrong with that. Nothing wrong if taken in moderation and it doesn't destroy your life. Can religion actually destroy life instead of promoting it? Our first tendency to answer that might be to look at other religions with which we strongly disagree and point out how those religious systems mislead their followers. Let's begin with an easy example.

Jonestown Revisited: Most would agree the spiritual society created by Jim Jones in the 1950s and that ended in tragedy on November 18, 1978 was an evil religious addiction. Charismatic leader Jim Jones influenced people wherever he traveled. He and his "People's Temple," the religious organization he founded in 1955, were influential in electing George Moscone as mayor of San Francisco in 1975. He met with political celebrities, Governor Jerry Brown, Vice President Walter Mondale, and First Lady Rosalynn Carter, to name a few.

Jones preached "religion is an opiate to the people," and steered people away from Christianity to his form of socialism. Looking back at those events, we wonder how 918 people could lose their lives to a religious zealot who so controlled their minds that they would follow him anywhere, even to their deaths. But religious addiction has a mind-altering effect on its followers.

There are those who, after having smoked for years and finally quit, become the loudest and often most obnoxious opponents of smoking. To put it in religious speak, they have "come to the light," "seen the error of their ways," or "been born again."

That pattern follows even more intensely in religious addiction. Don't get me wrong, change is often good, but when it spills over into "I'm okay" but, "now you need to change, too," it infringes on our comfort zone and our freedom to "come to the light" in our own time and in our own way.

For alcoholics, drug addicts, and others who destroy their lives through their addiction, a measure of rescue may be appropriate. Part of the success of Alcoholics Anonymous is their Twelfth Step—to take their message to other alcoholics. The victim becomes the savior. Sponsors open their lives to other alcoholics while often maintaining a relationship with their own sponsors for years.

Had the tragedy of Jonestown been thwarted at the last moment, a twelve-step program to bring the members out of their blind faith to the teachings of Jim Jones might have restored them to a balanced religious/spiritual belief system. But, the idea of sponsorship may have been too overwhelming for most. Why put faith in another individual when that was what got you into trouble before? No, the victim-savior scenario would have needed modification.

To substitute one addiction for another yields only a measure of health. Smoking is better than alcoholism, so some people give up the bottle and take up the coffin nails. Overeating is better than smoking, so people binge on donuts, candy, and cake. Religious addiction is better than all the others, so I find a charismatic leader and a body of believers who love me and follow them blindly wherever they lead—even to Jonestown.

Religion as a Drug: How can religion/spirituality be seen as a drug?

1) It gets you high: Many are attracted because of an altered state of consciousness. I've felt this high in times of worship, in the singing of songs, and in the sacraments. Others experience it by speaking in tongues, being "slain in the spirit," or by ascetic practices such as fasting, flagellation, and sweat lodges. Some experience religious highs in prayer, meditation and contemplation. These are only a few examples of the "highs" that religion can provide. In moderation, these are wonderful experiences.

2) Inability to think for yourself: One problem I faced with my birth religion was the inability to veer from its doctrine. If I questioned something about the religious institution or the Bible, and if no real answer was available, I was often told to "have faith." A measure of faith is healthy, but blind faith to a religion or to an individual can prove disastrous—as was shown with Jonestown's Jim Jones and other religious self-proclaimed messiahs/saviors throughout the centuries.

3) Strict adherence to a set of rules: Everything becomes black and white. No gray areas. No room for discussion, compromise, or a change of beliefs. The Bible/Qur'an/Bhagavad Gita/Book of Mormon, or whatever is claimed as ultimate truth, is the only true word of The Divine. Insistence on strict adherence to observances such as a specific way of life, a strict dress code, worship rituals, and nutritional adherence is often demanded as well.

4) Judgmental: Addictive religions often make fun of other religions, pointing out their gross mistakes in conduct, and beliefs, and predicting their destruction if they don't come to the true light. No one measures up to their standards, except perhaps their religious guru. They find fault in everyone.

5) Inability to cope in the real world: Relationships become strained. One example of this occurs in marital relations when one is a "believer" and the other is not. The "believers" are often dogmatic and rigid in her or his beliefs to the point that family members and friends tend to stay away when possible.

6) Split personality: Putting on a happy face around others, but being mean or obstinate in more familial situations like work or at home. Treating others differently as if they had a work personality who degrades those below them, and a spiritual personality who loves everyone—everyone, that is, who believes as they do.

7) Savior mentality: I am right. You are wrong. I must therefore save you before it's too late. This can apply to an individual, for example Jim Jones, or a religious organization.

8) Unreasonable financial giving: If you sell your home and give the money to a religious organization, chances are you've gone over the edge. What is or is not appropriate in giving to a religious assembly varies, but a good rule of thumb is that when you are not able to pay your bills because of your religious generosity, you need to rethink your beliefs. If you believe that to give to a religious organization is the only form of spiritual contribution you can make, you may also need to rethink. Giving to the homeless, to food banks, to disaster-relief funds, to a family or friend in need——but not to the detriment to your primary obligation to your own and your family's financial well-being—are all legitimate forms of giving.

9) Predicts the end of the world. The Rapture, the Great Escape, the Second Coming, the end of life as we know it, the destruction of the world through nuclear war—all the scenarios that have predicted the end of the world have failed to come true. In the past, every time a religious leader has predicted a specific date for the end of the earth, that prediction failed. Even predictions by sources not necessarily religious in nature have been mistaken. We survived the year 2000. My wife and I kept the Y2K shelves for years. We considered replenishing them for the world's end on 12-21-12, but never got around to it.

10) Fear-based: Predicting the end of the world is a form of fear-based religion. Pure religion should promote positive qualities such as peace, harmony, gentleness, courage, strength, and above all, love. Any religious group that tries to scare people into their way of thinking instead of loving their flock into a personal relationship with The Divine has the potential for religious abuse.

11) Proclaims to have a direct connection with The Divine: This one is tricky, because most spiritual leaders have had a connection with The Divine. The test is in the messages they receive and pass on to their followers. Do the messages go against common sense? Do they go against traditional beliefs? Do they require their followers to do something dangerous, unethical, or immoral?

12) Judgment is more important than mercy: Some religious leaders claim to believe in a merciful divine other, but teach that this God figure will condemn people to eternal punishment unless they are one of the chosen, or forgiven, or select—all depending on their beliefs—and only those few will make it past a divine being of judgment and into their ultimate state of eternal bliss.

I have provided twelve symptoms of religious/spiritual addiction to guide you. Later we will consider thirteen steps to help those who seek recovery from religious abuse. If I were to choose the symptom I consider the most important it probably is the inability to think for yourself. In the Peoples Temple, 918 believers lost the ability to think. They followed blindly, and like rats trailing the Pied Piper, followed Jim Jones to their deaths.

Chapter 8
STRENGTHS OF RELIGION

"Religion is the means.
Divine Love is the Goal."

We have taken a look at religious abuse. It's only fair to consider the positive effects of religion. After all, why do billions of people believe in some form of Ultimate Being? In a sense, I'm basically claiming religion to be a positive side effect of spirituality. People were spiritual long before religions told them how to be. Spirituality, the ability to find The Divine, is the ultimate goal of religion.

A Moral Code: Socrates defined morality as "how we ought to live." Religions have sets of rules to guide behavior. Some are more elaborate than others, but these moral codes establish a basis of behavior that allow societies to function. Without them, life falls into chaos. Because most religions have the golden rule as part of their teaching, many of society's moral codes are built upon that concept.

At times, religions fail to provide proper moral codes, and when that happens, deeply religious/spiritual individuals speak out to change the rules to a higher standard that discriminates against no one. Notice that many times these leaders have been highly spiritual, and that it was their religion that guided them to a higher standard.

A Place of Community: "You wanna go where everyone knows your name—and they're always glad you came"—from the TV show, *Cheers*. Some of my fondest childhood memories are times at church, being with people I knew, who knew me, and who were glad I came. Religion builds community. It provides a place of safety and a time to relax, unwind, and enjoy shared likes. Ideally, religious experience is all inclusive, but in reality, it sometimes fails.

Still, the ideal is the goal, and many religious organizations are achieving a high rate of success in making community a reality. As religious gatherings grow, one problem is the growth itself. When the organization ministers to hundreds and even thousands, it becomes difficult to know everyone's name.

Successful groups recognize that keeping a sense of community is vital to the spiritual health of their people, and so they devise small groups that cater to special needs.

Perhaps we could create a religious gathering based on the Cheers theme song, building into it the qualities that make a local bar attractive.

- Everyone goes to relax and have fun.
- Someone is there to listen to your problems without judging you.
- We go there when we are lonely.
- We go there when we want to celebrate.

- We go when we feel down.
- We go when we feel good.
- We don't have to pretend to be happy.
- We don't have to dress, act, speak, or think in a specific way.

Not every bar can claim all those qualities just as not every religious experience can claim to be that open and accepting. But, we need a place to relax, meet friends, and be at peace with The Divine and with ourselves. Places of worship can provide that atmosphere.

A Start: Another positive aspect of religion is its ability to give us a start. We may complain about the particular form of religion we were assigned to upon our arrival on this planet, but nevertheless it was a launching point. I doubt that a return to my birth religion will occur for me. But, I am grateful for the beginning, the guidance, the information—right or wrong—and an initial introduction to The Divine.

Fond memories of church abound. One Sunday evening, when I was young, my father asked if I'd like to go forward when the altar call was given. If you're not familiar with church-speak, an altar call is an invitation to kneel at the altar at the front of the church and make a commitment to God. The commitment entailed confession of sins, request for forgiveness, and the acceptance of Jesus into your heart.

Being young, I didn't have a lot of sins to confess, but those I could remember were offered with heartfelt sincerity. A peace settled over me that evening that I'd never known. I didn't want to move from that spot or lose that feeling.

There is healing in the act of confession, and although I assess the experience differently now, I treasure my introduction to the spiritual world. The following Sunday, when the minister invited people to come forward, I looked to my dad for permission to return for another dose.

I was addicted. Hopefully, in a good way. I wanted the high of the previous week. This scene played out for several weeks until one Sunday my dad whispered, "You don't have to go every week."

Slightly disappointed, I nodded and stayed put. But the seed had been planted and the quest for God had begun.

Sometimes it's possible to get too much of a good thing. Church attendance was required by my dad for two and a half hours on Sunday morning (Sunday school and a worship service), another two hour and a half hours on Sunday night (including Youth Group meetings), an hour on Wednesday night, and an hour and a half on every night of revival services, which lasted from Sunday to Sunday. I was never enthusiastic about homework, but on revival week I'd ask to stay home to do my homework.

Vehicle for Change: In all those hours of church attendance, things sunk in. The Bible stories, the Scripture memorization, the teachings, the doctrine, and a moral code. All good things to know and to live by. Not that the church always lived up to what it professed, but eventually I learned to separate the church, the leaders, and its teachings. I accepted the good and discarded the rest.

I lived in a bubble of beliefs, mostly good ones, which formed the world around me. It wasn't until years later that I formed my own opinions about the world and other religious belief systems. Imagine other children in other countries being raised in similar ways. Born into a predetermined religion—usually the one most prominent in their country—they form their view of The Divine based on what is taught them.

Our world view is expanding. If our birth religion has prepared us, we can take the most important fundamental teachings and compare them with other world views. Similarities come to surface—love, peace, kindness, gentleness.

Religion has the potential to create massive positive change if we can set aside our differences and accept that all roads will eventually bring us home. Unfortunately, it also has the potential for destruction. Promoting guilt, shame, exclusivity, narrow-mindedness, and rigidity keep us separated from our brothers and sisters.

For a short time, I worked as an associate minister. A bus ministry was one of my assigned duties. The idea was to offer pick up and return service for children so that they would be able to attend Sunday school and children's church. When special children's programs were presented, their parents were invited to attend. Who wouldn't want to see little Johnny star in a play or musical?

An introvert by nature, I pushed myself to go out and play the Pied Piper. One of my young recruits was a winsome young African-American. Excitement ran through me as I watched my new recruit exit the bus and head for class. My excitement ended the next day when the minister approached me.

"Wayne, we have to be careful not to recruit too many of those young boys."

"Why?"

"I understand you want to reach out and help, but I'll not lose my church."

Puzzled, I stared, waiting for an explanation.

"I have a friend who started recruiting black kids, and after a while his congregation complained. Eventually his regular members stopped coming and he was left with the poor black kids."

At the time, I was young and naïve. Disappointed, my zest for bus ministry fled that day and recruitment became a chore I dreaded. A few months later I resigned and returned to my hometown. Unable to find another church needing a disillusioned assistant pastor, I found work in a different field.

In the past, some religions have been behind the times in helping to create positive social change. Some religious assemblies promoted segregation and preached that slavery was a part of God's plan.

This discourse has momentarily pulled us away from the point of the chapter, but it reminds us that religious organizations are run by humans, and sometimes we make mistakes.

Let us glean the good. Let us keep our eyes and hearts open. There is not one singular, infallible religion, and if we keep our eyes on leaders and institutions and not The Divine, we can get detoured on our road home.

Chapter 9
RELIGIOUS AGAIN?

"Healing comes in all forms,
including spiritual healing.

But, how do we heal when
religion inflicts the wounds?"

My Story: In the early '90s I returned to the ministry and served on staff with my local church. I served for three years and near the end of that time my marriage of twenty years was in trouble. Divorce was eminent, so I resigned my position and returned to my previous job.

Sure enough, my wife and I divorced in June of 1994. The pain of that event affected us deeply. My pain was intensified by the reaction of the church. Part of the problem was, no one was prepared for it, and they didn't know how to handle the situation. My church attendance slowed before the divorce and ended after it. I no longer felt comfortable in the religious institution I'd grown up in.

The church is not to blame for my divorce or my initial pain. But, knowing their reaction and feeling their condemnation brought further shame and suffering into my life. Their solution was not acceptable, their cure ineffective. Still, I believed in God— the word I used to refer to "The Divine" in those days—and I sought to stay on the path.

I was still an ordained minister, but attending that particular religious gathering or another one of that denomination felt uncomfortable. Searching for alternatives, I tried other forms of Christianity, but eventually left each one disappointed. Even the newer, more liberal churches with their contemporary music, casual approach, and upbeat messages failed to satisfy for long.

There was nothing wrong with the religious gatherings—they were, after all, made up of individuals trying to find their own ways, just as I was. They didn't know how to help, and besides, my journey was meant to take me down different trails. Eventually the home-based religious gathering I described in chapter four, Bedside Baptist: Church of the Inner Spring, became the place I attended on Sunday mornings, Sunday evenings— in fact, every day of the week. Discouragement overtook me, and I gave up. *I'll just call myself a pagan and be done with it,* I thought.

Christianity had shown me one part of the elephant, but I was blind to other views and impressions. That phase of my life, when I attended no established religious gathering, allowed me to do some preliminary healing. But, ten years after my divorce, an event occurred that set my recovery back.

I received a letter from a minister connected with my birth church. He held a position in the denomination's hierarchy, and part of his responsibilities involved checking up on wayward ministers. After a formal greeting, he said my divorce and non-involvement with their denomination had come to his attention. He wanted an explanation. My ordination was on the line.

Although I had left his denomination, I had not given up on God or religion. I had written and published Christian books about the nature of God. I had taught and spoken at Christian writers' conferences. I shared some of these things with him, but apparently he was unimpressed. In his reply he quoted large portions from the denomination's Manual—their second Bible. I needed to submit myself to a panel of ministers for evaluation. I knew of ministers who had gone before the tribunal with lesser transgressions. Their fate was rarely kind.

With no doubt in my mind as to the outcome of their inquisition, I declined, and tendered my ordination credentials.

He never contacted me again.

The pain of that "defrocking,"—for that is what it felt like—caused old feelings of inadequacy to resurface. I wasn't good enough. I had made mistakes. In their vernacular, I had sinned. Even though their doctrine spoke of love, forgiveness, and restoration, I knew that road would be long and hard. I didn't think I'd ever be free from the whispers and the judgment.

I remarried and fortunately my new wife, who had a different religious background, believed in me, comforted me, and reassured me. "You *are* good enough," she would say. With her love and understanding, the healing began again. Whenever situations bring that period of time into my memory, I still feel a small portion of the pain, even though I've forgiven them and myself as best as I can.

I now accept and can even appreciate the actions of the minister whose communications led me to release my ordination. At the time I felt a part of my essential essence had been taken away. But, it opened the door to new experiences, new beliefs, and a greater compassion. Five years after that loss, life brought an experience that shook my world—but this time for the good.

New Age: My wife, Linda, and I planned a vacation to see the Grand Canyon in the fall of 2010. One of Linda's friends suggested we spend some time in Sedona, Arizona. I had never heard of Sedona, but quickly learned it was considered by some to be the New Age mecca of the West. Seven vortexes were supposed to be located in the area. *What the hell is a vortex?* Psychics could be found on every corner. *On every corner and in between the corners.* And, New Age shops carried books, crystals, holistic healing remedies, more psychics, strange New Age music (strange to me anyway), and Tibetan crystal bowls.

If Shirley MacLaine had visited Sedona, she would have thought she'd died and gone to New Age heaven. But, for a former Christian minister who had known nothing except fundamentalist doctrine, I was overwhelmed. Not necessarily in a bad way, however. I was like a kid at Christmas, looking at all these strange gifts and thinking, *Somewhere among all the trappings there has to be something I can play with.*

Like a kid, I unwrapped those gifts and gave each a try. Some felt strange. Others felt comfortable. Most seemed puzzling. We ventured up a hill that was supposed to have a vortex near the top. We were told to look for a tree whose trunk and branches were twisted. I searched for a tree that fit the description and stood by it. Nothing. I touched it. Still nothing.

I wondered if it were the correct tree. I asked Linda to stand close also. Again, nothing. I felt as if I'd unwrapped an empty Christmas box. No gift, not even a note to say "Batteries not included." We made our way down the hill and returned to our motel. It was perhaps my first New Age disappointment, but it wouldn't be the last.

As time went by, I learned to accept the experiences without judgment. But just because I didn't sense the stream of energy flowing around the tree didn't mean it wasn't there. The one benefit I noticed from the experience, however, was how calm and peaceful I felt. Could it be that the energy affected me in that way? I didn't know then, and I don't know now.

People are moved in different ways, and we learn to accept that what touches one may not have meaning for another. That's another good reason for having different world religions. I have experienced times of great ecstasy through worship. I've witnessed others who sat near me in the same worship service and, at least by outward appearances, were not affected at all.

The same has proven true for me. I've attended many services that moved others to tears while I sat waiting impatiently for the speaker to finish so I could go on with my day. Were we listening to the same speaker? Or did they secretly have their ear buds in so they could listen to someone else?

What Am I? Did my exposure to the New Age make me a New Age convert? I don't think so. In fact, I'm not sure I can tell you what class of religious belief I fall into. I'm a collection of all, a proponent of all — and sometimes none.

I haven't found the perfect religious belief system. Nor the perfect teacher, preacher, or human being. I'm told that some came close, the Buddha, Jesus, Mohammed, and others, but I don't know any of those people. I only know what others have told me about them. How do I know the information is accurate? My birth religion would tell me to just have faith. If I were born a Buddhist, or Muslim, or Taoist, my coreligionists might also tell me to "just have faith." So, the question is, have faith in which one?

After studying a few of the world religions, not a scholarly study but more an experiential study, I connect with most of what I've learned. It's not so much book knowledge as it is the heart knowing—a feeling that resonates inside. I like many of the teachings of Siddhartha Gautama, the first Buddha. I embrace some of the teachings of the New Age movement, but not all. I'm enthralled with the words of the Bhagavad

Gita[16] and believe they contain great wisdom. The "Tao Te Ching" has also proven to be a powerful and effective guide.

At the same time, Bible passages memorized years ago return to bring me comfort and encouragement. I still have strong Christian leanings and appreciate greatly my background there. I may dismiss some of the doctrine and some of the customs, but the wisdom still influences my life.

I discovered something else in this eclectic collection of religious beliefs. Many experiences I thought were strange in religions that I had never explored can also be found in a similar form in Christianity. For instance, the Bible speaks of prophecy—the ability to foretell future events. In several of the religious gatherings I have attended, the idea of messages from the spirit world was presented. Some claimed these messages to be from relatives who had passed (mediums), others from spirits or guides, and still others claimed their messages were from The Divine, the Holy Spirit, or God.

Being a natural doubter, I often shook my head in disbelief. Until, that is, I discovered that the messages often proved true. How could they know that? People made life-altering decisions based on the messages they received. This was true in the New Age type religious gatherings and also in some of the Christian groups.

Each of us has different abilities. Prophecy doesn't seem to be one of mine. I do, however, have an inner voice that guides me when I listen. New Age calls it intuition or psychic impressions. Christianity calls it the Holy Spirit or the voice of God. They might argue that my inner voice and intuition/psychic impressions are not the same. They might even argue that someone who listens to intuition or psychic impressions is actually listening to the devil.

Let the theologians argue and work it out. The end result is what's important, and using different, seemingly opposing words to describe the same experience doesn't alter the experience.

Re-Ordained: Following my heart, in 2012 I received ordination from two different religious institutions. After having felt pressured to tender my minister's license once before, I figured it wouldn't hurt to have a backup. Being a licensed minister simply means I can perform weddings, funerals, sacraments, and all the other duties pertaining to the ministry. Did I need it? No. But, I wanted it. I don't pastor a church—nor do I intend to. Currently I speak at three different gatherings—usually not on the same weekend. That meets my needs. Someday I might speak to larger crowds, but the size

---

[16] The version of the "Bhagavad Gita" I am familiar with is the "Bhagavad Gita For Beginners: The Song Of God In Simplified Prose" [Kindle Edition] by Edward Viljoen

doesn't matter. I'm spiritually connected like never before in my life, doing what I love, and helping people.

In my heart was the knowledge that only The Divine can grant or revoke ordination, and that The Divine willingly grants to all who seek. No paperwork needed. No battery of tests or interrogations to pass. The Divine knows the heart.

I shall retain my ordination for as long as needed—and hopefully no one asks me to surrender it again. I immensely enjoy performing weddings, and they also add to my fixed income. However, one does not need to be ordained to be a spiritual person. I embrace the religions of the world and find value in each view of The Divine they present. If there was such a thing, I'd prefer to be ordained by a yet-to-be-incarnated religious organization, the "World Order of All-Religious-Beliefs-Are-Valid Gathering of Spirit-Directed Believers." We would meet in abandoned church buildings, mosques, temples, shrines, stripper pole dance studios, bars, nightclubs, and in the fields, by the streams, and on the beach.

We would celebrate times together and times of individual worship. We would sing, meditate, pray, contemplate, and, most importantly see each other as Divine children of The Divine Light—and we would love one another as the brothers and sisters we are.

I know. The name needs a little work. I'm not sure I could fit it onto a billboard.

Chapter 10
"THE RELIGIOUS RECOVERY PROGRAM"

"Take what you like, and leave the rest."

–A Twelve-Step Saying

Recovery: For a period of about fifteen years, beginning with my divorce and ending around 2010, I wandered in religious obscurity, not knowing how to heal from the hurts, not knowing who to turn to, not finding compassion. Never a drinking man, bars weren't a place for me to unburden my sorrows. Two lines from a Negro spiritual described my feelings, "Nobody knows the trouble I've seen, nobody knows my sorrow."

Perhaps my pain seems minimal compared to yours—and you may be right. For me, however, my world had been devastated—and what made things worse, was feeling that I had no one to blame but myself. I wanted a safe place to unburden. For a while, I attended a twelve-step program to help me deal with the life-choices one of my children had made.

I found there the qualities lacking in my religious circles. Acceptance. Understanding. Forgiveness. Release of old beliefs. Hope. Love.

A paraphrase of the *Cheers'* theme song comes to mind. "Wouldn't you like to go where everyone knows your name, and they don't care what baggage you bring? Wouldn't you like to go where love envelops the room, and the bright light of love touches every heart?" That place was not within my grasp, nor within the grasp of many others who have traveled a similar path.

But, what if it were? What if it were possible to create a safe place where religion was set aside for spirituality? Where heart emotion was more important than black-and-white rules? Where people treated you with respect, even if they didn't know your name until the minute you walked into the room?

Al-Anon taught me that such a place exists. If it works for alcoholics and those affected by alcoholics, for overeaters, for drug addicts, and for others suffering from addiction or its consequences, then why can't it work for those of us hurt, disappointed, or abused by religion or the religious?

It can, and it will.

Religious Recovery: Consider what it would look like to have a twelve-step program to help recover from religious abuse. If I'm not opposed to religion—and I'm not—then how do I justify the creation of such a program? Because, like it or not, religions have injured people since their inception. Some injuries are more severe, such as when leaders sexually abuse children trusted to their care. Some are less severe but still leave wounds that need to be healed.

A religious institution is much like a family. Some are good, others not so much. The leader fills the mother/father role, and the members of the flock make up the family. Because the leader and the flock are made of imperfect humans, injuries happen. Sometimes it's a leader who inflicts the injury and sometimes it's a member of the flock. But, consider the role of the leader. What happens when religious leaders are hurt, disappointed, or abused by the religious institutions they serve?

I worked in organized religion long enough to see the men and women behind the curtain claiming to be the spiritual wizards—the great and powerful Oz figures. They were mortal, and I saw plenty of imperfections. Sometimes they felt their religious gatherings had failed them and that they were trapped in a set of beliefs—things that could not be questioned without fear of discipline, possible dismissal, and/or defrocking.

An institution they'd given their lives to, and now felt was wrong, could take away their livelihoods, their reputations, and their ability to find similar work in their chosen field. All at a moment's notice.

Where do ministers go for healing? Who listens to their pain? How devastating and degrading it is to face life without your identity. We need a place and a gathering where anonymity is practiced, where leaders can cast off their robes and their titles, and be accepted as simply John or Todd or Sally or Leslie.

The place I'm speaking of may not attract men of the cloth. Perhaps a few. But, those who have lost their way and feel that religion is to blame will gather to share, to encourage, and to heal. Just as other twelve-step programs are designed to meet specific needs, Religious Recovery will help those who want to find their spiritual path with or without the aid of a religious institution. Some may seek healing in order to return to their birth religion. Perfectly okay. Others may question the rules and regulations and want guidance to a different path. Also perfectly okay.

The meetings will be open to any who feels they have lost their way, been misguided, or are simply looking for a broader understanding of The Divine. As in twelve-step groups, the use of the words "should" and "ought" will be discouraged. Agnostics, atheists, and people of all religions will be welcomed. During open discussion time, those who want to speak may do so. A moderator opens the meeting. He/she may introduce a topic or share a reading and say a few words about the topic or the reading.

Acceptance of other religions and other beliefs is the cornerstone of the group. Cross talk is inappropriate, but sharing after the meeting is appropriate as long as it is done in the attitude of "take what you like and leave the rest." It's always better to begin by saying something along the line of "This is my story, maybe it will help someone."

Differences: Religious Recovery differs from twelve-step groups in several ways. Religious Recovery has thirteen steps instead of twelve, and thirteen "stones" instead of the "Traditions" of A.A.

Although some who attend Religious Recovery may have a religious addiction, we do not believe that "once an addict, always an addict." Following Buddhist teaching, we believe in the middle way, or moderation in all things.

Religious Recovery does not pass out coins commemorating progress. Only the individual can know when healing has occurred. A specific number of attendance days doesn't indicate spiritual healing and growth. The better indicators are Divine-like qualities—love, acceptance, wisdom (love coupled with knowledge), compassion, and others. Personal benchmarks as measured by the individual may be shared and celebrated. We do not discourage progress, we simply allow the individuals to determine personal goals and accomplishments.

Religious Recovery also does not encourage or discourage the sponsor system. Some people have put their faith in a religious leader who abused them in some way. We do not encourage the replacement of one spiritual leader with another—no matter how well-meaning that person may be. Ultimately the goal is for each to become a minister unto herself or himself. To discover their own paths, and to lead by example. Friendships may be formed and some of these may have the elements similar to sponsorship. As long as inappropriate dependence doesn't develop, these friendships can be mutually beneficial.

The victim-rescuer relationship also needs to be guarded against. Broken people sometimes see themselves as victims. They have been hurt by the institution of religion, by a family member, by a spouse, by a friend, by an employer, or by a stranger. Let the love and acceptance of the Religious Recovery program be the platform that allows for The Divine to rescue. We steer our faith and trust away from individual leaders and institutions and put the focus back on that which is greater than self.

By embracing and pointing the way toward The Divine and not ourselves, we avoid the victim-rescuer circle. When someone falls into the role of rescuer, it's difficult to move beyond it. The role plays to our egos. Our proper role is to be a facilitator—a role that cannot include our egos.

As with twelve-step programs, we discourage direct advice during meetings. A participant may share a situation from his or her life that has brought pain, and confide not having known what to do. Instead of giving direct advice, each person responding shares from personal experience what has worked for him or for her, couching the statements with the sentiment, if not the actual words, "This is what worked for me, maybe it will help."

Those who share speak to the group and make no more eye contact with any one individual than they do with anyone else. When one-on-one eye contact is made, the person seeking solutions may feel pressure from the group—real or imagined. By addressing responses to the group, the attention is taken away. The attention is centered back onto the basic topic—religious hurts, disappointments, abuse—and is addressed as if it were presented anonymously.

Meeting Structure: Please bear in mind that these are guidelines—not rules or commandments. We do not want rigid structure and we don't want to form a new type of religious institution. We might call Religious Recovery the un-church, but we do so somewhat in jest. We do not want to construct physical buildings, become a money-grabbing organization or a political entity. Our purpose is spiritual healing, growth, and reunion with our spiritual world family. We are a gathering of wounded individuals who want to get back to the basics of spirituality.

Volunteers fill the role of moderator. Their job is not to control the meeting except to steer it back on course if the discussion goes astray. In the infancy of forming a new group, there will often be a need for one person to fill the role of moderator on a fairly regular basis, but if there are at least two or three attendees the role can be rotated among those who are not intimidated. Still, someone may need to fill the role for weeks before another person feels safe enough to help share the load.

Meetings start and end on time whenever possible. The suggested duration is one hour. Meetings begin with the ringing of a bell, the playing of a Tibetan bowl, or any other form of non-offensive signal. The moderator introduces himself or herself with "Hi. Welcome to Religious Recovery. My name is _____." The group responds with "Hi (or Hello) _____." Last names are not needed. No religious titles are shared. The concept of anonymity applies both to the ones giving their names and the ones hearing them. Many people who want to heal from religious abuse don't want to know if there's a minister, priest, shaman or monk in the room. Their fear of judgment may surface, and the ability to share can be stifled.

Religious attire would be best left in closets at home. No one is exalted over another at Religious Recovery meetings. We are all seekers after Divine wisdom and truth. We all have something to give and something to receive. Our combined efforts bring strength, power, and light.

We strongly discourage the specific mention of religious leaders or organizations. A leader or organization that failed one person might be the specific leader or group that could provide spiritual guidance to another. We do ourselves and others harm by degrading an individual, a religious organization, or a denomination. Religious Recovery was not founded to be an organization to pass judgment on the success or failure of others. Even speaking of individual leaders and religious organizations in a positive manner is not encouraged. The concern is one of coming across as an evangelist for a particular religious group or leader. Agendas such as trying to gain converts must be abandoned.

There is the advice of, "If you want to avoid conflict, avoid talking about religion or politics."

Remember the safe topics and a lot of conflict will be avoided: love, peace, patience, kindness, understanding, compassion, acceptance, gratitude, and more. We repeat these often to help us remember. Our goal is not to convert—only to present. We share what has become meaningful in our lives and allow others to present the same. They may find help in our words; we may find hope in theirs. Openness and acceptance of one another bring about the desired results. Narrow-minded and ego-centered talk will slow progress and present detours. The goal is to bring additional wisdom and light which can help us see the path clearly and help us avoid potholes, slippery slopes, and unnecessary detours.

After the moderator gives his/her name and welcomes everyone, a moment is taken to explain the importance of anonymity before asking if anyone is visiting for the first time. If visitors are present, additional emphasis may be given to the importance of anonymity. Visitors are presented with a copy of the "Newcomer's Guidelines" and a few minutes are taken to briefly go over the information. The moderator may give special emphasis to the concept that whatever is said is merely the speaker's opinions, and no one can claim absolute truth.

Talking about religion, except in general terms, is avoided. Talking about spirituality, however, is encouraged. Finding a balance between the two, challenges us to new levels of understanding.

Once the preliminaries are finished, the moderator shares a topic for discussion or announces an open forum and reads a portion from *Every Path Leads Home,* or from one of its companion works, or a similar work that embraces the concepts of Religious Recovery and addresses the chosen topic. Following the reading, the moderator might briefly share his or her insights from the reading, remembering to couch the words with something like, "This is what the reading means to me," or "This helped me…"

Once the moderator has finished—usually about ten to fifteen minutes—the floor is open for discussion. People introduce themselves with first names only before sharing what is on their heart. Because the meeting is open to all beliefs, the gatherings are not closed with any particular prayer. However, the following generalized closing may be used if so desired:

"I am part of Divine creation. I honor all my brothers and sisters. I honor their road and their beliefs, and will endeavor to share loving acceptance with all I meet. As we share our journeys, we learn from one another. May The Divine guide us and always be at our side."

Members may hold hands if the atmosphere seems conducive. Hugs are encouraged as well as the invitation to return and to bring any friends they feel might benefit.

Disputes, altercations, and disagreements should be met with loving kindness, returning peace for any form of perceived attack. One goal of Religious Recovery is to find a way for religion and spirituality to coexist. This can be accomplished if we strive to bring a deeper spirituality to religion so that those who say they are "spiritual but not religious" may discover it is possible to be both. To accomplish that goal, our meetings must avoid conflicts by seeking common ground and capitalizing on the positive benefits found in both religion and spirituality.

Chapter 11
THE THIRTEEN STEPS

Step One

"We recognize we have been hurt, disappointed, or abused by religion or the religious."

We Recognize We Have Been Hurt: We begin by recognizing the need. Not just the outward symptoms, but the inner brokenness that allowed for outside elements to bring pain and suffering. We search our hearts and minds for commitments to manmade institutions instead of Divine connections established within the inner sanctum of the indwelling Presence.

We recognize we are spiritual beings created by Divine Spirit. When the Divine is our parent-teacher-guide-lover, we find protection from hurts and strength to live by Divine power.

Blaming a person or institution is easy. Accepting the responsibility for our own path requires courage. Others can guide us, but only so far. We must find our way in the dark. Light is there for the asking. Seek it within.

As a youth, I felt a stirring to follow a spiritual path. I cloak those words now in spiritual language. At the time my language would have said, "I felt called to the ministry." The meaning behind those words would show you a young man influenced by his father, the minister of his church, and Billy Graham. I saw myself standing in front of throngs of people who were waiting to hear my eloquence, and who would flock to the center of the stadium to make a commitment to Jesus. To this day I admire the work of Billy Graham, and had my life turned out to be similar in any way, I believe it would have been rewarding. He has championed the cause of spirituality and helped thousands of people.

My life appeared to be heading in that direction. Involved with my church youth group as president and self-appointed spiritual guide, I jumped at the chance to join a new group called the Impact Team. The concept was to form a choir of Christian teenagers from the church district to tour other churches on Sunday mornings. We hoped to make an impact on teenagers and encourage them to make a commitment to Jesus. Those on the team who "felt a call to ministry" were also given the opportunity to preach the Sunday morning sermon.

The team would arrive on Saturday evening, practice, share an evening meal prepared by members of the church, and spend the night with a local family. Once, when it was my turn to preach, I was supposed to spend the night with the local minister and his family. His home was within walking distance of the church, and for some reason I was in that home earlier on Saturday, probably because they'd prepared a snack or meal for us. When we drove to the church that evening for practice, I familiarized myself with the return route.

When the rehearsal was finished, we were paired with our host families and were transported to their homes. Since I knew how to get to the minister's house, I asked if I could stay behind awhile to study my sermon notes and pray. I assured him I remembered the way, and he agreed to let me stay.

Darkness fell while I was preparing, and when I was ready to leave, my sense of direction that seemed so sure earlier in the day suddenly felt uncertain. Before long, I was lost. Strange city, long before cell phones, no map, no way of knowing which way to go, I became concerned, then scared, then terrified. I did the only thing I could—I prayed. Then bartered. "Please, God, if you just point me in the right direction, I'll promise to…" I don't remember what I promised that night. I only hope God forgot, too.

Following on the heels of bartering came begging. As I walked blindly in the darkness, first trying this road, and then that one, my pleadings flowed with deep sincerity along the river of my tears.

Finally I reached a spiritual crossroads. For a short period of time, I lost faith. There was no God. No Higher Power. No Divine Other. I reached the point of anger, and I challenged The Divine. "God, if you really exist, then get me out of this mess! And, if you can't, then I no longer believe in You."

My tears continued as I tried to calm myself. I didn't know what to do. Alone and afraid, the only solution that came to mind was to stick out my thumb and take a chance that in the late hours of a Saturday night I wouldn't be picked up by a drunken sex offender.

The first vehicle pulled off the road and waited for me to get in. I strolled uneasily to a rusty old pickup truck, wondering what awaited me. Opening the door, the man asked where I was headed. Hoping my red eyes couldn't be seen in the dim light of the cab, I explained my situation. I didn't even know the address of the minister's home.

He knew where the preacher lived and offered to take me there. I sat in silence, and my rescuing angel spoke not a word. Upon delivery, I thanked him; he nodded and drove away.

My faith in an unseen force—call it God, or Krishna, or Jehovah, or The Great Spirit: it doesn't matter—my faith grew beyond measure. I had trusted in my own ability to find the way home, but when that ability failed, I searched for help from beyond my physical strength. The man and his truck felt like an angel and his heavenly chariot.

The problems of a lost teenager may seem small, but my crisis of faith was heard and answered by the Overseer of the universe in a way that restored my beliefs.

Religions fail, spiritual leaders disappoint, and our struggles are often misguided, but within the soul is the gyroscope of Divine Love, Divine Guidance, and Divine Power. When we think we have lost our way, that gyroscope reminds us: every path leads home. Trust, search within, and it will take you there, even if the mode of transportation is an old pickup truck.

Hurt, Disappointed, or Abused: I share but one example of being temporarily disappointed in my connection with The Divine. The disappointment came when I felt I had to beg to get the attention of The Divine, and that my spiritual belief in prayer was nothing more than childish imagining. It took what seemed like a small miracle to restore my faith. I can share other examples from my life in which religion or the religious disappointed me. Religious abuse resonates mildly with me, but certainly not as much as others, especially those sexually abused by a spiritual leader.

We all have stories to share. No spiritual path is without pitfalls. Perfection has yet to be found. The recognition of the hurt, disappointment, and abuse is the place to start. The recognition that we want to move beyond religion to a place of spirituality that is independent of institutions and people is the direction that moves us forward.

Step Two

"Come to believe that The Divine has no religion,
is greater than religion, and can heal us from our hurts."

Greater Than Religion: The recognition that The Divine is greater than religion must be more than mental assent. Our hearts feel it, our spirits know it, and our intellect follows. Religions attempt to define the undefinable. Attempts to see the un-seeable.

The power of the sun can sear the eye's retina if viewed for too long. If we imagine The Divine as a light ten times brighter than the sun, then no mortal could look upon it. The only way to gain a short glimpse would be to view it indirectly, perhaps through a dark mirror, or by reflecting the light through a telescope and onto a sheet of paper. But The Divine is more than Light, and the true essence of its Being cannot be seen with the human eye. Occasionally, if we try hard enough, we may get a glimpse of its magnitude and feel in our hearts its essence.

If we share those glimpses with others, and they share theirs with us, we put together a fuller picture. We may never come to a full understanding, but we can have a bigger picture and a better appreciation. However, if we think our picture is complete and make a religion out of our beliefs, we shut ourselves off from further knowledge and understanding. The Divine is greater than religions.

Can Heal Us: We need spiritual healing. This is not a case of positive thinking. The illness is misguided religious beliefs. Although some physical illnesses respond to the power of positive thinking, spiritual illness responds only to spiritual healing. It does incorporate positive attitudes and positive beliefs, and in some ways it's self-healing, but ultimately we turn to The Divine to do for us what we cannot do for ourselves.

We may, when we are physically ill, try to cure ourselves with a variety of home remedies, but if those fail and the sickness seems out of our ability to cure, we seek "professional" help. Often the professionals find ways to allow our bodies to heal naturally, with only slight assistance from other remedies. And when that doesn't work, then modern medicine is available.

When we are spiritually ill, we may try a variety of things to restore the spiritual balance. If nothing succeeds, we often turn to a religious group or a spiritual leader. At times, they are able to assist. When they are not able, and in fact, when their proposed solutions seem to worsen the illness, we have no place to turn but to The Divine. Truth is, even when spiritual leaders suggest something that works, they are not the ones performing the actual healing. The Divine works with and through them to guide us to the healing of Divine Spirit, and The Divine restores the individual to full spiritual health.

From Our Hurts: Divine healing removes the pain of disappointments, hurts, and abusiveness. The Divine works with us through the power of forgiveness to remove these ailments as we'll see in the thirteen steps, but the issue here is what draws us back to wholeness. We can be restored to spiritual health through the power of Divine Love.

Step Three

"Recognize that we are spiritual beings and decide to turn our lives over to 'that which is greater than self,' referred to in these steps as 'The Divine.'"

Spiritual Beings: The essence of religion and spirituality centers on the fact that we are more than flesh and blood. Without the spirit, or soul if you prefer, life is meaningless. We live, we die. No more, no less. Why bother with anything else? Some believe the spirit lived before birth. Some believe it never dies. Some believe the spirit has lived through many incarnations. Religious Recovery does not tell you what to believe. No judgments are made as to which path is right or wrong.

We do, however, agree with the basic premise of having a spirit or soul, and that the acceptance of that premise separates us from trees, animals, and non-sentient beings. Because we are able to perceive, experience consciousness, have subjective experiences, and dream (both literally and figuratively) there is ample evidence to claim we are spiritual in nature.

The physical cloaks the spiritual, but the importance of the spiritual surpasses our short-term earthly existence.

Decide to Turn our Lives Over: We alternate between two beliefs: we decide to live as if there is no Divine presence, or we decide to live as if there is a Divine Other. We may try both paths and even bounce back and forth between them. We look around only to discover other people struggling with meaning and purpose. Implanted in our character is the search for something outside the physical that can unite with our spirit to provide the missing pieces of the picture.

Religion waltzes in with answers. Some satisfy—at least for a time—some do not. Turning our lives over to someone, some concept, or to some unseen Divine Presence can be a frightening decision.

To That Which is Greater Than Self: Many have turned their lives over to that which is equal or less than themselves. Blind devotion to a religion or a charismatic leader can lead to disappointment, anger, hurt, and bitterness. When we turn our lives over to that which is greater, beyond, and above ourselves, we yield to the driving Force of the Universe. To the nature from which we were created. To the Divine spark that brought into being the universe and all that is around and within us.

Referred to as The Divine: Many twelve-step programs refer to "that which is greater than self" as Higher Power. In Religious Recovery we use the term The Divine. The name is not important. Some use Brahma, Rama, Krishna; some say Allah, Yahweh, Buddha, Jesus; others might say Ahura Mazda, Queztalcoatl, Biame, Jupiter, Zeus or Breged. All are efforts to name the Nameless One. All, in one way or another, point to the belief of a Higher Existence or a greater all-encompassing being that gives life, breath, and meaning to our presence.

They also share another thing in common. They claim to have a way that points back to The Divine—to have a path that leads home.

This step begins the journey, or in some cases, resumes the journey. Losing our way is more of an illusion than reality, but at times the reminder of what we are is needed. We are spirit. Some would say we are spirit with a capital "S." Certainly the essence of being is connected to Divine Spirit, was created by Divine Spirit, and returns to The Divine.

Step Four

"Accept that this Higher Power is understood in different ways and by different names in various religions and cultures, and open our lives to hearing the Divine Voice in any way it chooses to communicate to us."

Different Ways and by Different Names: In step three we considered some of the formal names by which The Divine is known. The list does not include the less formal names used to describe The Divine—names that give an indication of the different ways religions and cultures understand Higher Power.

Abba, used in Christianity was made popular by Jesus. It translates as father, and the two words are often used together as in "Abba, Father." The expression is an intimate term and can best be thought of as "Daddy." For Jesus to describe The Ultimate Being as Daddy irritated many of his contemporaries, but it brought into existence a different way to view The Divine. Think of God as the ultimate Father with all the positive attributes—loving, caring, comforting, providing—but with none of the negative traits.

Many Native Americans view The Divine as an omnipresent, invisible, universal force. They celebrate the Earth, Air, Fire, and Water. Hinduism and Buddhism often add a fifth element, that which is described as beyond the matter. "Beyond the Matter" is another understanding of the Divine Presence.

We may also hold views of The Divine that have not served us well. An angry god, a jealous god, or a vengeful god. Can our view of The Divine evolve? Certainly we can change the image we hold of The Divine. That doesn't change His nature, but by changing our image we might be able to bring what is truer into our understanding. We understand that when we use words like "he/him/she/her" to refer to The Divine, we do so because it's easier than repeating the phrase "The Divine" over and over. Even though some don't see The Divine as male or female, many still view Him/Her as having both feminine and masculine qualities.

Open Our Lives: We return once more to the example of the blind men and the elephant. Each man had a different experience of the elephant. All were partially true, but none painted a complete picture. In step four we accept that the different ways and different names are images of the same thing. We open our lives to hearing, understanding, and accepting different world views, incorporating them into our evolving perception when possible, and rejecting them without prejudice when they don't seem to resonate with us.

Any Way He Chooses to Communicate: The Divine has many ways to communicate. By denying the validity of different roads, we cut ourselves off from many of these forms of communication. By deciding that The Divine speaks only through one book, one leader, one religion, or one nation, we limit Divine Spirit's power, omnipresence, and even love in our lives. In fact, The Divine is not limited in power, presence, or love. What is limited is our ability to perceive, as if we're seeing through a glass dimly and believing ours is the only glass.

Step Five

"Share our struggles with others of like-mindedness
trusting that our anonymity will be guarded by all."

Share Our Struggles: Finding others of like-mindedness is not difficult. In preparing this work, I often mention to people the concept of starting a thirteen-step program for religiously abused, hurt, or disappointed people. Most people laugh. One person I asked about the laughter said she laughed because she didn't think I'd have trouble finding people to attend.

The idea hadn't occurred to me that many, perhaps even most people, at one time or another feel hurt, disappointed, or abused by religion or the religious—including, but certainly not limited to, religious leaders. Religions set up rules or guidelines to live by. Breaking those rules creates the occasion for "The Keeper of the Rules" to call into question our behavior. Which is a politically correct way of saying; we are judged and found guilty.

Depending on the severity of the crime, the punishment and restitution can be simple or severe. Gossiping is considered a minor offense and often carries little or no correction. Murder and adultery often demand expulsion and the loss of one's religious credibility. Most transgressions and their punishments fall between these extremes.

In sharing our struggles with the group, however, we do not gather to blame, defame, or complain. A simple telling of the details is sufficient. The purpose of the group is not to grumble over what happened, but to share in order to grow through the experience and beyond it. To forgive ourselves and others. No judging is accepted at Religious Recovery meetings. Our goal is not to judge but to heal.

Our Anonymity Would Be Guarded: Without anonymity, our meetings fail. We trust our brothers and sisters to keep our secrets. Using first names only at meetings helps create a safe environment. Creating friendships often helps heal, but use discretion in sharing too much personal information until you feel completely safe.

Step Six

"Take inventory of ourselves to discover any way
in which we have hurt, disappointed, or abused anyone by our religious beliefs."

Take Inventory of Ourselves: We begin the healing process by turning our gaze inward. The idea of taking inventory permeates the twelve-step programs, and it finds additional usefulness in Religious Recovery. Taking stock of our selves is healthy. A Native American proverb says, "Great Spirit, help me never to judge another until I have walked in his moccasins."

I cannot know the reasons and motives for why someone did something to me, but I can know the reasons and motives why I did something to someone else. Most of the time when I hurt someone it wasn't intentional. Something I said or did might have been misconstrued. Nevertheless, we wound people with our words or actions. Before accusing someone who hurt us, we try to understand our own agendas for hurting them or someone else.

The principle of "what goes around comes around" is at play here. First we stake stock of our own lives. Doing so provides a measure of grace, forgiveness, and understanding. We don't want to mete out accusations based on perceptions. No one knows what is in the mind of another. Look within. Check your own motives first, and do not judge another until you've walked in their moccasins.

Hurt, Disappointed, or Abused: Our goal is to heal ourselves, and to restore relationships with leaders and organizations whenever possible. Occasionally, a word said in haste or in jest injures another to the point they will not accept our apology. A quick check within to determine if we have been guilty of the same thing will aid in recovery. Time usually allows for grievances to settle to the point where an apology can be offered and accepted—but not always.

When the hurts go deep, we offer time, distance, understanding, and love. We forgive ourselves and pray that others will one day forgive us.

By Our Religious Beliefs: We want to be right. With doctrine and a divinely inspired book to back our position, we boldly share "The Word" that will save the world, denying the authority of any other book claiming to be divinely inspired, and arrogantly thrashing any other religion that doesn't believe as we believe, act as we act, or sing all of the stanzas of the songs in our divinely inspired songbook.

We have no idea the damage inflicted by our well-meaning but often misguided zeal—until we discover the damage inflicted on us.

The reason we take inventory is to make amends to others, but also to be in a position where we can heal ourselves.

Step Seven

"Choose to forgive those who hurt us in the name of religion."

Choose to Forgive: Notice that forgiveness is a decision—a choice. We can choose to withhold forgiveness, but ultimately that decision stifles our spiritual growth, emotional harmony, and mental stability.

Forgiveness is difficult, and when it involves religion, the decision becomes more challenging because we have placed our faith and trust in the church and its leaders. We trusted that they would speak from love and always have our own best interest in mind. Often we are not able to separate a leader from the religion, and we discard the entire package.

Imagine—before the days of the GPS—that you asked someone for directions to Disneyland. That person assured you that she or he knew the way, and would take you there, guiding your every step. "Don't worry," the person would say, "I know what I'm doing. I've been there before. Follow me."

You put your trust entirely in that individual and listen carefully to the directions—what to do, where to turn, and what to avoid. Days, weeks, and months go by, and still no sight of the Disney promised-land. Finally, your car dies in the desert, miles from gas stations, restaurants, and lodging, and your guide says, "Well, I better be going." Furious, you lash out in anger. "Where the hell do you think you're going? You said you'd take me to Disneyland."

"Disneyland? I thought you said desert land." Your guide gets out of the car and vanishes into the distance.

Religious leaders are mortal beings filled with the frailties that makeup all humanity. The Disneyland guide's incompetence may have been unintentional or it may have been malicious, but does it matter? The result is the same.

Had we stopped to ask others for directions before we began our journey, we might have discovered more than one route to our destination, and we could have decided for ourselves if we wanted to take the short route, a longer more scenic route, the northern route, the southern route, or the middle way. We could have considered stops along the way—national parks, state parks, relatives or friends we might have wanted to visit.

Putting our faith blindly into one guide didn't bring us to our destination. Our disappointment is increased by our loss of time and money. If we believe the deception was intentional, our pain deepens.

We choose, instead, not to forgive our guide. We hold onto our disappointment and let it fester. It grows from disappointment to anger and eventually rage. The guide moves on—oblivious to our feelings and having forgotten the incident. If confronted, that person may show no remorse, rationalizing it was a simple misunderstanding.

After a while, we make our way out of the desert. We have a new traveling companion whose name is Bitterness. He goes with us everywhere we go. He troubles us during the day and also during our sleep—and he won't go away.

Finally, after a wearisome journey, you arrive at Disneyland. Your expectations soar again, but with a pang of regret. Something isn't quite right, and the park experience fails to live up to your anticipation.

You look back at what went wrong, and once again you blame your guide.

Several mistakes can be pointed out: putting blind faith in your guide, ignoring your intuition, and, when disappointment came, failure to forgive and move on.

The old expression: "forgive and forget" is not realistic. We are human, and the ability to wipe our memories clean is not within our abilities. Nor should it be. The memory serves a purpose. If you fail to fix a leaky faucet you will probably receive a large water bill. Memory reminds us not to let that happen again.

Work with a guide who promises to take you to Disneyland but who leaves you stranded in the desert, and your memory will remind you to choose your guides more carefully in the future. Instead of "forgive and forget," the expression needs to be "forgive and forgive—and forgive, and forgive…" Not that we allow the hurts, disappointments, or abuse to continue. Memory reminds us to stop and move on. Great hurts, however, require a greater resolve to forgive.

When memory brings back the incident, it often brings back the feelings. Each time it does, we commit again to forgive and let go. With each recurrence we make the decision once more to forgive.

In the Name of Religion: When you deal with religion and its leaders, you deal with life directions. Our goal is to find a way from this realm of existence into the next. Decide to separate leaders from their organizations. Seek wisdom from within. Ask if the organization the leader represents is still a valid road, or if the organization also misguided your steps.

Make the decision to forgive the leader and the organization. Through forgiveness you heal and move on. If you need to, choose another road. When you refuse to forgive, your journey becomes laborious instead of fun, and when you finally arrive at the destination, you may discover a measure of disappointment. Not so much disappointment in arriving home, but in not realizing that the journey — the anticipation — was supposed to be part of the excitement.

Step Eight

"Seek forgiveness from those we hurt unless doing so would cause further harm."

Seek Forgiveness: Sometimes you're the fly, sometimes you're the swatter. Sometimes you are hurt, other times you do the hurting.

On our spiritual journey we play follow the leader and also lead the followers. We are guides to some, tourists to others. When our leaders and guides disappoint, we forgive them. When we mislead followers and tourists, we seek their forgiveness.

In writing this book, I realize the overwhelming responsibility I've taken by assuming the voice of leadership. If my words lend hope and comfort, I'm grateful. If they hurt, I'm sorry and I ask forgiveness. Please trust that the hurt was unintentional.

I believe what I write, but that doesn't make it right. I admit my weakness, and ask you to weigh carefully the advice and "take what you like and leave the rest." I offer my words with an open heart and I encourage you to test the words and decide for yourself.

The Buddha taught for forty years and then encouraged his followers not to believe anything he said unless and until they investigated for themselves.

We seek forgiveness in our lives in other areas, but for the purposes of Religious Recovery we concentrate on our attempts not to be misguided, and not to misguide. We hold our wisdom up to the Light, knowing that truth withstands, but deceptions fade away.

Unless Doing So Would Cause Further Harm: Sometimes it's best to leave well enough alone. I knew a man who felt remorse for the way he lived his life, and when he approached the end decided to confess his mistakes and seek forgiveness. Adultery was top among his regrets, and so he confessed his infidelities to his wife.

Perhaps she knew of some of his infidelities, but many she was unaware of. The confession may have felt good to him, but it proved devastating to her. At a time when she was about to lose the only husband she'd ever known, he confessed his unfaithfulness with several women. Her ability to grieve his passing was tarnished by his betrayal.

What benefit came of the confession? Even though he was dying, she felt like the fly, and he was the swatter. Her capacity to comfort him in his last days was diminished as she fought to forgive him for living the way he did, and for dying without taking his "sins" to his grave. Better he had left his mistakes to The Divine's forgiving grace.

Seeking forgiveness must be balanced by any damage that could be done. Confession is more for the one confessing than the one being confessed to. I recall Jimmy Swaggart's confession after his sex scandal was discovered. Whether his confession was genuine is not for me to judge. I hope it was. But, was his confession appropriate or did it do more damage than good?

His behavior disappointed millions and hurt his family, toppled his ministry, cost people their jobs, and critically hurt his credibility. Was it appropriate for him to confess publicly? I don't know. Perhaps if he had confessed quietly instead of airing his laundry, things might have turned out differently.

It is with grave caution that we consider the ramifications of the hurts we inflict. If Jimmy Swaggart listened to the voice of The Divine in his decision to confess the way he did, then I trust his decision. If his motives were guided by anything less, then his confession was misguided. Shortly before his misconduct, he had judged a fellow evangelist, Jim Baker, and called him a cancer on the body of Christ. Jim Baker, however did not retaliate, but said he found no joy in Swaggart's predicament.

Those who trusted Jimmy Swaggart as their spiritual guide were hurt by his fall. Many forgave him and remained loyal. Others forgave, but looked for a different guide. Some forgave him but left him and the denomination that had sponsored him. Some refused to forgive and left that particular religious gathering and its parent organization, and also abandoned their belief in God—their word for The Divine. Their path home took a detour.

When we, like Swaggart, are the flyswatter, we need to search for spiritual clarity and seek forgiveness. Swaggart might have served the ministry better if he'd confessed, sought forgiveness, turned the ministry over to another, and quietly gone away, at least for a period of time.

The guiding principle of step eight is this: Do no harm—which also means: Do no further harm.

Step Nine

"Forgive ourselves for all harm we may have caused, even if it was well-intended."

Forgive Ourselves for All Harm: Forgiving others is sometimes easier than forgiving ourselves. Because I grew up with strong ties to religion and a desire to be a spiritual leader, the pressure for me to be perfect was ever present. Sometimes pressure came from my parents, sometimes from my church family, and sometimes I applied it myself.

"Sins" were defined as missing the mark, and I often missed the mark and even the target. During the years prior to, during, and after my divorce, the pressure placed upon me for perfection took a massive toll. I had let down my family, my friends, my church, and most of all myself. I let down The Divine, too—or so I thought. How was I to recover? Feeling like an outcast in all my familiar settings, I withdrew from my normal routines and sought refuge in solitude.

My children were my main concern, and I maintained a relationship with them as best as I could. It wasn't easy. I'd hurt them, and they needed time to heal before they could forgive me. As far as my spiritual relationship, I struggled with the reaction of those who had supported me. They didn't know how to handle the situation any better than I did. We stumbled around, felt awkward most of the time, and did the best we could.

Church attendance slowed to a Holiday rate—Christmas and Easter, and an occasional Mother's Day. I took time to think, to contemplate what had happened, where I went wrong, and whether there was any way to recover.

Reading spiritual books stopped for a time. Prayer was hit-or-miss—usually miss. Meditation was gone. In spite of all the heartache, frustration, pain, and guilt, I knew the Creator of the Universe had not given up on me. I knew that my problems, as big as they seemed, were solvable. I didn't know how or when, but I knew in time my traumatized world would end and a new life would begin.

The new life began in small ways. I placed one foot in front of the other and did the things that had to be done: eat, work, and repeat the cycle. People went on with their lives. A few reached out to me. Some forgave, others didn't bother. All went about their own worlds, business as usual.

It wasn't until years later that I received a better understanding of the power of forgiveness. Under the care of a different leader, one who saw the suffering I carried, I was offered spiritual healing in the form of forgiveness. We talked about the past, and she helped me to see things differently. I was able to forgive those who hurt, judged, and condemned me.

Most importantly, I forgave myself. There is perhaps no greater mistake than withholding forgiveness from others or from ourselves. When we refuse to forgive, it returns to us in judgment, pain, and imprisonment. We are held captives in anger, hatred, and bitterness. When we refuse to forgive ourselves, it holds us in a vice of negative thoughts and feelings.

Even If It Was Well Intended: We conclude this step with the words, "even if it was well-intended," almost as if it were a footnote. If our actions were well-intended, why do we need to forgive ourselves? Many times people feel their intentions were good, but sometimes their good intentions bring catastrophic results. Just because we meant well, doesn't mean the pain isn't real if our good intentions went askew.

Consider a woman who decides to do some matchmaking. She sets up her friend with a man she thinks would make a good match. In the beginning, her prediction goes well. They hit it off, eventually get married, and build a life together. Then suppose this woman discovers the man she recommended to her friend has become abusive: verbally, emotionally, and physically. She regrets her meddling and feels guilty. Her intentions were good, but the result played out badly.

The matchmaker feels she has failed her friend, and considers all the abuse her friend suffers at the hands of her husband to be her fault. If anything were to happen to her friend, she feels she would never be able to forgive herself.

Feeling responsible, she interferes again in the hope that she can convince her friend to leave her husband. Well-meaning again, we can imagine how this, too, might go wrong. The decision could force her husband's hand, and death or disfigurement could result. Maybe the husband had seen the error of his ways and decided to seek help, but before he could find a counselor, this meddlesome friend's actions caused him to panic.

Our first thought may be for the woman to mind her own business, but that, too, could go wrong. The point is, no matter what we do, we make mistakes. We are not perfect. We forgive those moments when we act out of poor motivations: greed, anger, hatred, jealousy, and so on, but we must also forgive ourselves of those well-meaning moments when everything went terribly wrong.

Step Ten

"Seek tolerance and, when possible, accept all religious faiths without judgment."

Seek Tolerance: Tolerance is the first step toward peace. We take it deliberately. We make the decision to open our minds to differing opinions. What makes us so cocksure that our religion, our minister, priest, or shaman is the only one connected to The Divine? What makes us so sure the religious gathering we've belonged to all our lives has a monopoly on who the Creator is and how we are supposed to live?

Why can't we all get along? I continue to ask that question, and the answer comes back again and again: because we all think we are right—therefore everyone else must be wrong, and we'd better fix them. But, in our efforts to fix them, they are trying to fix us. I'm reminded of a saying that goes, "I love you, you're perfect—now change."

Tolerance opens the door to peace: among the nations, among couples, within families, and within our hearts. When we no longer feel the need to be right, it frees us. We tolerate differing opinions. We have our own, but we no longer feel the need to persuade another.

Even though tolerance is the first step towards peace, it isn't an easy one. I'm not asking you to change your beliefs or give up your religion. I'm not saying, I know the way—follow me. No. And I won't. You might be right. I might be right. We might both be right, or we might both be wrong. All tolerance asks is that you consider the possibility—as remote as it may seem—that there might be more than one way. That other roads might get you to the same destination, or that those roads, even though they may not work for you, might work for your brother or sister.

When Possible, We Accept All Religious Faiths: The key word is "possible." What or who determines whether it is or isn't possible? Each individual must decide what is possible for him or her to accept. Once more we forgo the question of right and wrong. To try to establish guidelines for what is appropriate and what is not brings us back to the role of judge. Some religious belief systems may seem ludicrous, and—from our point of view—wrong.

Earlier I described several different religious assembly styles. Many of them I personally experienced. My goal was to be open-minded in an effort to find the treasure within each one. After my experience I discovered the ones where I felt comfortable with the leader, the flock, and the teachings. Those particular gatherings met my needs—at the time.

At times I've also considered religious gatherings that didn't seem to meet my needs, and I was tempted to pass judgment or perhaps even laugh at what was going on. Then I noticed the way the flock was positively affected, and I said to myself, "Who am I to judge?"

That's what tolerance is about. Allowing all of us, individually, to search and discover the roads to The Divine that meet our needs. In addition, if those roads stop meeting our needs at some point, we also tolerate and accept each other's decision to find and blaze a new trail.

Without Judgment: We come back to this concept. No judgment. We accept all decisions, from many gods to one to none, and by whatever name or names. We accept without judgment wherever a person stands and walks. This is the key to peace, and more importantly the key to having a heart of love. As long as there is love in our hearts, we can tolerate differences of opinion. When we have love, we don't have to be right. We don't have to judge. We simply accept. All will work out the way it's supposed to. Love your friends, your enemies, those who believe differently from you, and be at peace.

Step Eleven

"Seek through prayer, meditation, and contemplation to improve our relationship with The Divine, praying for clarity of mind, an open heart, and further ways to heal ourselves and our world from the abuses of religion."

Seek through Prayer, Meditation, and Contemplation to Improve Our Relationship with The Divine: Simply defined, prayer is talking to The Divine, meditation is listening to The Divine, and contemplation is a combination of both. A lot is written about prayer in the Christian community, almost to the exclusion of meditation and contemplation. I confess my own exposure to meditation didn't happen until I read *Celebration of Discipline* by Richard Foster. The book came more than twenty years before my venture into the realm of spirituality as I now understand it.

Foster opened my eyes to a new way of communicating with The Divine—listening. I also questioned the value of my prayer life. It seemed like all I was doing in prayer was telling The Divine what The Divine already knew. I marveled in the discovery that I could hear guidance and direction through meditation, although it was a far cry from the practice as those in the Eastern religions understood it. I wonder if they struggle with prayer the way we struggle with meditation.

Still unknown to me was the practice of contemplation, at least by definition. Everyone practices contemplation to some degree. When we look at a sunset, we contemplate the power of the force that created the sun. When we scan the stars at night, we consider the magnitude of the heavens and the littleness of man. In those moments, The Divine whispers to us. Our unspoken prayer is, "Who are You?" The answer differs according to the needs of the individual. But, even the silence of heaven speaks.

When I left my birth religion and found spirituality, I discovered the power of these three keys of the Universe. The Divine guided, nudged, and prodded me, leading me into the practice of forgiveness and to other like-minded individuals. My connection with The Divine grew stronger, and my heart softer.

Listening doesn't come easy for many people. Sitting cross-legged on a zafu meditation cushion felt eccentric in the beginning. My wife was skeptical and quick to tease. Over time I came to look forward to the practice, knowing it was an opportunity to listen for Divine guidance. My life ran smoother, stress decreased, and work became easier.

The main point in the beginning of step eleven is to appreciate the value of these practices in moving from religious rules to a spiritual relationship—yes, a relationship with The Divine, but also an improvement in all relationships in life. Many will find one form easier than the other two, and will naturally spend more time with that practice. That's perfectly acceptable. Each personality needs to be sensitive to what works best. I strongly recommend, however, that we develop all three practices and spend time each day communicating with the Ultimate Creator.

Praying for Clarity of Mind, An Open Heart, and Further Ways to Heal: The more time we spend with the practices, the more clarity our minds receive. In meditation we seek to quiet the mad monkey mind. In contemplation we seek to open our hearts. Meister Eckhart wrote, "What a man takes in by contemplation, that he pours out in love." In prayer we seek forgiveness that we may heal ourselves and heal our world—through forgiveness.

Wisdom is knowledge coupled with love. Through contemplation we acquire wisdom. Through wisdom we know intuitively the loving thing to do. Power is courage coupled with wisdom. Not the world's power, but the power of The Divine. Not power to change circumstances, but power to change lives. Power, wisdom, forgiveness, and love combine to create peace both personal and global.

These practices, if done consistently, reshape our thoughts, our emotions, our lives, and our world. Religion takes a backseat to the power of a man or woman who prays, meditates, and contemplates.

To Heal Ourselves and Our World from the Abuses of Religion: Personal healing and growth form the launching pad of Spiritual deployment. As individuals across the planet build their spiritual arsenals, we prepare for a nonviolent spiritual coup to bring peace to the Earth.

Before we join this army of peacemakers, we must first make peace within—healing our hurts, disappointments, and abuses from religious people and religious leaders, as well as from those who claim no religious or spiritual association. Anyone can hurt us if we let them, but healing is simple: Forgive and be forgiven. Heal others by forgiving any and all grievances, and you will be forgiven and healed. Here is a simple affirmation you might try.

"I forgive, I receive."

In the act of forgiving, our hearts open to receive. When we refuse forgiveness, our hearts close.

Years ago, my wife and I arranged to meet several couples for lunch after church. The group grew as we invited additional couples after the service. We chose a neighborhood restaurant, arrived, and gave our name and the number of people in our party. We chatted as we waited, catching up on church and family news. I'm sure a sprinkle of gossip flavored some of the conversations.

Time slipped by as we watched more and more people being seated ahead of us. Having just come from church, no one was quick to complain. After all, weren't we supposed to forgive and overlook minor infractions? The minutes turned to an hour, and then an hour and a half. People who had arrived after us had finished eating and left while we still waited to be seated.

Patience turned to irritation, irritation to resentment, and eventually resentment turned to anger. Finally, we were called. Someone on the staff knew we had been mistreated because I overheard a specific waitress had been assigned to serve us, one who was known for her ability to pacify disgruntled customers.

As we took our seats, apologies were given by all staff members assigned to our tables. The miracle-working waitress added her apologies and also said the management extended their apologies and wanted to offer us free desserts.

Anger overtook me at the injustice of their behavior, and I said bitterly, "No thank you!"

Cooler heads than mine were present, and a friend said calmly, "Thank you, that would be nice."

I love desserts. Some days I live by the philosophy, "Life is short. Eat dessert first." To allow my bitterness to take away something I loved was idiotic. By refusing forgiveness I blocked my ability to receive. My friend's wisdom humbled me and embarrassed me, but in a good way, because I learned a lesson that day. I didn't master it because it has come back from time to time to remind me that withholding forgiveness blocks my ability to receive.

I forgive, I receive. That day I received a dessert. Something sweet, something that made me happy. Spiritually, when we forgive we receive a multitude of blessings from The Divine and from our brothers and sisters.

Healing the world begins and ends with the same principles of individual healing. When we forgive, we receive. Some see forgiveness as weakness, but it is ultimate strength. Some see forgiveness as too easy, but it is difficult and requires great courage. Some believe forgiveness solves nothing—but it solves everything.

By the end of World War II, America had lost many sons and fathers. Our suffering and pain were intense, and we could have chosen to concentrate on our own pain and loss. Instead we poured out our wealth to other nations and chose to forgive our enemies. We supported and were deeply involved in the healing not only of ourselves but also of the world. Our forgiveness and selflessness propelled us into the most abundant and successful nation in the history of the world.

When the power of love, forgiveness, and the golden rule are lived by individuals and nations, the basis for the healing of religious abuse and the healing of any and all abuses becomes present to the global community. As we will discover in a later chapter, spiritual healing through acceptance, forgiveness, and love also has the power to heal the world's religions and bring a peace that will encompass the planet.

Step Twelve

"Having recognized the difference between religion and spirituality, we strive to be true to the Spirit within all of Divine Creation and to be a Light to point the way."

Having Recognized the Difference between Religion and Spirituality: Step twelve returns us to the beginning—distinguishing between having a form of religion, but denying the power of The Divine. We have used the term spirituality to define a lifestyle that is dependent upon a connection with that which is greater than self.

We do not judge religions as good or bad, right or wrong, spiritual or unspiritual. We accept all religious paths, but recognize that what works for one person, may not work for another. Personal preference and growth as determined by a deeper connection to The Divine form the basis of each individual's decision as to what religion is personally the right religion, what religious gathering is right, and what spiritual guide(s) will best meet her or his current needs.

At the same time, we recognize not only the potential for religious abuse, but the reality of its presence whether intentional or unintentional. Our goal is healing. Restoration to the same spiritual path may be possible, but we also believe other paths may prove beneficial, even if the road moves away from traditional religion into new areas of spiritual awareness. We also believe in the benefits of distancing ourselves from organized religions. Many spiritual masters spent time alone, often for weeks or months at a time.

We understand the difference between the terms religion and spirituality, but we also see value in both. The community of believers (religion) offers support, teaching, guidance, fellowship, and worship. Spirituality offers an inner connection with The Divine that, at times, seems missing from religion. It offers personal spiritual growth and peace.

We Strive to Be True to the Spirit within All of Divine Creation: The Spirit of Divine Creation is the same Spirit that lives within everyone. Each individual contains a spark of divinity. Whether we fan that spark through spiritual practices is what freewill choice is all about. To deny the spark in others, just because they fan their spark differently than we do, dims our ability to see their spark and tends to hide our spark from their view as well.

To be true to the Divine Spirit means to recognize we are in this together—for better or worse—and the best thing to do is learn to get along. Simplistic, yes, but ironically, though one essential goal of religion is to teach us how to live together in peace, all too often, religion becomes the source of our fighting.

Our mission begins in the quietness of our bedrooms, our meditation spaces, and our home altars. We become a light to point the way by connecting to Divine Light. Once we accomplish a connection to The Divine our essence becomes our message. When we leave our quiet place and go about our daily lives, our Light goes with us. There is no need to proselytize.

We only need to be.

Step Thirteen

"We follow the principle that when the student is ready, the teacher will appear. The witness of our lives is the only message we need to carry to others."

When the Student Is Ready, the Teacher Will Appear: If the message of Religious Recovery is divinely inspired, there is no need to proselytize. There is no need for missionaries to go out and make converts, no need to knock on doors, pass out flyers at airports, bus stations, and malls, and no need to leave tracts in bathroom stalls. If the message is not divinely inspired, a quick death would be kind and appropriate.

The Witness of Our Lives: If our lives—the way we live, the way we treat people, the way we respect and honor all sentient beings—are our witnesses, then words become secondary. There is no need to convince people of our beliefs, or to try to persuade others to think as we think, act as we act, or worship the way we worship. When we live in accord with The Divine, the difference will be noticeable and people will approach us. At that point, we offer them any wisdom (love-based knowledge) based on our intuition that has been seasoned by time spent alone with The Divine. Never pushy. Never aggressive, abusive, or overly assertive. After all, we don't want to drive anyone away. We don't want anyone to be in need of a program to recover from this Religious Recovery program.

This final step also has two implied applications. First, we recall that we were, each of us, once the student, and when we were ready, our teacher appeared. In time, someone may come to us in need of our light, and we then become a teacher sharing with those in spiritual darkness. Second, we are still students, and when we are ready to go even further along the path, the teacher/master will appear. That teacher/master may be another traveler, but it may also be the Spirit of The Divine. In this way we understand that all who participate in the program alternate between student and teacher, between guiding and being guided.

Chapter 12

THE THIRTEEN STONES

The thirteen steps help us heal from the hurts, disappointments, and abuses of religion. As such, they deal with things that happened in the past. The thirteen stones take us deeper into spirituality and deal with the present moment. Each stone begins with an active verb and may be used as affirmations.

Stone One

*"**Assert:** I assert that I am responsible for my own spiritual path."*

Taking responsibility for their own journeys may be new to some people. After all, religious leaders and organizations have told us what is right and wrong—in fact, some have screamed their messages at us and even tried to scare us into believing the same way they believe. If we don't agree with them, we are judged, condemned, and sentenced to an eternal hell.

It's time to decide if we agree with their interpretation of the meaning of life, for that is what it is, their interpretation. They mean well, but they promote the same beliefs that were sold to them—often without doing any thinking on their own. You may decide to agree with them. But, you may not. Without considering other ideas and other beliefs, how do we know we've made the right choice?

It is not our goal to convince anyone of the rightness or wrongness of any religion. It is our goal, however, to point out the need to be open to other forms of spirituality. You may find your present religious assembly to be unfulfilling. You might want to consider other beliefs, other customs, and other roads to The Divine. You are in charge of the quality of your spiritual path. If you feel stagnant, maybe you've come to a dead end, and it's time to branch out.

Stone Two

*"**Open:** I partake of spiritual wisdom and knowledge*
from a variety of sources and open myself to different insights."

Imagine trying to make a cake with a recipe calling for only one ingredient—flour. Stir flour until flaky, pour into a cake pan, and bake at 350 degrees for 30 minutes. I'm not much of a chef, but I know the result would definitely not be a cake.

Some people treat their spiritual life in much the same manner, only one ingredient. But life is filled with many wonderful foods and each has a unique taste. Imagine eating one food for breakfast, lunch, and dinner, day after day, week after week, and year after year. Boring, yes, and not a healthy way to live.

Stone two encourages us to partake of the different foods that world religions have to offer. Try a little of this, see if you like it. Try a little of that—doesn't that taste good? Personally, I'm a meat-and-potatoes kind of guy. I try a variety of foods, but I usually come back to the basics of meat and potatoes. I was even a vegetarian for seven years. Although, if I'm being honest with myself, I was more of a junketarian. Yes, I gave up meat, but instead of replacing it with fruit and vegetables, I ate more junk food.

We may experience a similar path with our spiritual practice. For a time, I gave up on Christianity. I tried other things, dabbled in this and that, but ultimately came back to Christianity, although with a different understanding. And, I brought with me new spiritual foods from other sources that I discovered I liked very much. Christianity is still my meat-and-potatoes foundation, but my experience now encompasses a grander world menu.

We open ourselves to new experiences, new ways of seeing things, and new understandings.

Stone Three

*"**Question:** I question every experience, all information, personal motives—mine and others—including the ideas presented by Religious Recovery."*

Henry David Thoreau wrote, "Any fool can make a rule, and any fool will mind it." Even though I am open to other experiences, it doesn't mean I accept everything that comes to me in the name of religion or spirituality as ultimate truth. I question, doubt, mistrust, and have misgivings concerning new paths that claim to lead home. I am willing to try on new things to see if they fit, but I will also enter the experience with any reservation and hesitation that seem appropriate.

Many people have been deceived by religious charlatans. By carefully weighing new experiences and checking with my inner wisdom, the voice of reason and common sense, I filter out the paths that lead down rabbit trails and discover roads that keep me focused in light and love. I especially apply this approach to the information provided by Religious Recovery.

Stone Four

*"**Discern:** It is my responsibility to discern what works for me and what does not, always remembering that what may not resonate with me today may resonate at another time."*

Carrying the idea from stone three a little further, I discern the highest and best for my spiritual life. Often this is a matter of trial and error repeated by more trial and error. A spiritual concept presented in the teaching of Buddha, Krishna, Moses, or Jesus may not resonate with me today. Maybe I'm not ready to hear what is being said. Maybe I misunderstand what is meant. I lay it aside for now. The silence of my inner voice does not always mean there is no truth or spiritual assistance in what is said. It may mean that I am to wait.

The information may come to life at a later time, but it may never resonate with me. I accept that my road will never be exactly the same as another's route. I take responsibility for discerning what works for me, and for what doesn't.

Stone Five

*"**Connect:** Not only will I try to discern through mental activity, but I will also discern by connecting with The Divine through prayer, meditation, and contemplation."*

Mental activity helps us in many ways. I use common sense to guide me in many of my decisions, but in addition to common sense, I recognize other ways to discern spiritual truths. Three methods that provide spiritual guidance are prayer, meditation, and contemplation. I connect with The Divine, not only by reading and listening to spiritual instructions, but also by stilling the activity around me and going within to the spark of Divine that is my soul.

Each of these three forms of communication has its own strengths. By developing a consistent practice, I discover which of these forms works best for me, which one meets my needs, and which ones I need to develop more.

Stone Six

***Be:** Letting go of past hurts, disappointments and abuses, and letting go of future plans and expectations, I resolve to live in the present moment and simply be. Be present, be open, be available, be with Higher Self.*

The practice of living in the present moment is difficult. My mind drifts to past events, often with regrets or disappointments. When my mind drifts to the future, I often frame it through the eyes of the past, and so shape my future in ways I don't want to.

To be present, to be in this moment of time without thoughts of the past or future, that is a quality sought after by gurus and meditators everywhere. Our minds hold thousands of thoughts, and to be able to silence those thoughts long enough to listen to our Higher Self takes determination and practice. The essence of spirituality lies in finding that still small voice that knows instinctively where to go, what to say, and what needs to be done at any given moment of time.

Letting go of the past also entails forgiving ourselves and others of all grievances. When we fail to forgive, we carry those grievances into the present moment, and we also extend them out to the future.

Stone Seven

*"**Feel:** I allow myself to feel. My emotions are part of my being.*
By allowing myself to feel, I heal and grow."

I will feel. Feelings set us apart from other beings. I will not ignore them. I will allow myself to experience the gamut of emotions—even those feelings some deem negative. Emotions allow us to heal from hurtful situations, to learn, and to change when needed.

The positive emotions of love, joy, peace, kindness, contentment, and happiness provide opportunities for spiritual growth. I seek these emotions and choose to experience them, and, when possible, I endeavor to center my being in these emotions in an effort to share them with my brothers and sisters.

Stone Eight

*"**Release:** After experiencing all feelings, I release any emotions*
I deem harmful to my spiritual path."

I release all emotions that inhibit spiritual growth. I do this through forgiveness, meditation, and by asking The Divine to help me exchange negative, hurtful thoughts for loving, forgiving, healing thoughts. Even thoughts I deem positive can, at times, be harmful. Laughter has healing qualities, but when I laugh at someone instead of laughing with them, I may cause them pain.

I examine the feelings that show up in my life to discover if they are born of love or fear. I choose to let love guide me in dealing with my feelings. Whenever I make mistakes, I seek forgiveness.

Stone Nine

*"**Transform:** By changing my thoughts, I transform my life.*
I choose to change my thoughts concerning past experiences that hold me in pain.
I choose to see them from a higher perspective."

When I change my thoughts concerning a situation, I give myself permission to change my feelings and my life. I remember times when I felt anger and rage spewing out of me when I was in the middle of an argument. When that happens, after enough time has passed to give me perspective, I go back over the situation and examine it to determine what created those feelings. It's not long before I see the situation in a different light, and I am able to release the anger and laugh at my behavior.

What made the change? My thoughts created the incident, and I replaced them with new thoughts that turned a negative experience into a positive one. If we can see things the way The Divine sees them, we will laugh more, and fight less.

Stone Ten

"Harmonize: I look for the harmony in all spiritual belief systems and seek to add my voice to the music of the Earth. I seek peace with myself and with all people."

I find the things I seek, and when I search for harmony I find it. In the past I may have heard only discord among the world religions with little or no harmonious music to blend them together. I choose to listen for the music of the Earth, and if need be, to help create the song that blends us into one family.

I seek peace. The search begins with myself and extends from within to without. Being at peace with myself allows me to be at peace with others. Being in conflict with myself creates conflict in the world. Music has the potential to bring the world into harmony. I add my voice and choose to harmonize with life.

Stone Eleven

"Laugh: I choose laughter as the notes of my song.
This temporal life is a journey to be enjoyed.
I look for the comedy in situations, and I learn to laugh at my own comedy of errors."

The songs that bring peace and harmony to the world contain the notes of laughter. As I laugh, the world laughs. My life on this plane of existence is only a short journey. I choose to make it a fun ride and laugh at myself and my circumstances. The greatest weapons against hatred, violence, and war are love and laughter.

Mark Twain wrote, "Against the assault of laughter nothing can stand." Our world will not be united by religion, philosophy, debate, or mandate. Love and laughter are the weapons of peace. I will wield my weapons with reckless abandon.

Stone Twelve

"Thank: I am grateful. Gratitude helps me bring out the positive in my life and also makes room for The Divine to bring additional positive situations, people, and spiritual experiences into my life. I thank those who have guided me on my path."

If you want happiness in your life, learn the art of gratitude. And it is an art. We show gratitude and grace not only by the words we say but by the lives we lead. We thank people for their help and influence, and we pass it on by allowing positive change to make us better people. To live in a place of gratitude is to live in the realm of The Divine.

Many religious belief systems incorporate the practice of worship which can be as simple as paying respect and giving thanks to The Divine. Whether The Divine needs our thanks isn't the issue. The point is that when we offer thanks and live in gratitude, it improves our quality of life and our sense of wellbeing, and brings about peace. When in conflict with a person, finding ways to express genuine gratitude endears that person to us. It's difficult to stay angry when someone is telling you how much you mean to them and how grateful they are to have you in their life.

The same principle works with religions and nations. Discovering the positive, concentrating on similarities, and expressing gratefulness for those qualities breaks down walls and opens lines of communication and makes peace possible.

Stone Thirteen

"Love: I learn to deepen my ability to love when I learn to tolerate,
accept, embrace, and forgive. I choose to employ these attributes to my spiritual walk,
to my personal relationships, and to my world view."

Aristotle wrote, "Love is composed of a single soul inhabiting two bodies." I would add: Divine love is composed of the Divine Soul inhabiting all bodies. I recognize the love of the Divine Soul that inhabits my body, and I also choose to recognize that Divine Soul in the body of every individual.

Recognizing the Divine Love in all beings, I will tolerate, accept, embrace, forgive, and love myself and my brothers and sisters everywhere—no matter their beliefs. Every day I decide love is the way I will live my life.

Chapter 13
SAVING RELIGION

"For religion to serve humanity,
it must go back to its roots."

Tailor-made Religion: Religious organizations mold to fit the needs of current society. Rules change and doctrines are modified. Not long ago, eating meat on Fridays was forbidden by the Catholic Church. Now it is allowed.

In previous times Christian ministers in the fundamentalist movement used the fear of hell to keep their flocks in line and bring sinners to repentance. The mood and methods are changing. The current trend is to gain a following with a positive message—God is for you, He only wants the best for His children, you are entitled to be happy, healthy, and prosperous.

I prefer the new message over the old, but it seems we're losing sight of the middle ground and of the basic tenants of Christianity and religious intent in general. Motivating people through fear or financial gain might work, but the deeper issues—the middle ground issues—are world peace, personal peace, love, forgiveness, contentment, and the unity of the world family.

There are those who search and find the middle path, and their contribution is reshaping our thoughts and our world view. These people come from all religions, all lands, and all cultures. Their faith is simple but strong. Their vision is clear and full of Light. They are leading the way for spiritual renewal—a surge of The Divine that will open the eyes of the individual. We are reminded that we are not alone, that we are on a journey home, and that our search can—must—accommodate our brothers and sisters.

In time, religion will find the middle path. As they look at the important issues and release the need for micromanaging their constituents with rules and rituals, as they concentrate more on connecting with The Divine instead of funding their platforms, they will return to the basics of spirituality.

Religious Shift: Changing from manipulation to empowerment will be accomplished in small steps. Change must begin with congregations, and the change within the congregations begins with the leader(s) of the religious gathering—in most cases the presiding minister, priest, rabbi, or in the case of other world religions, the one who oversees the services. The focus moves from religious belief to personal relationships— both with The Divine without and within and also with our world family.

The shift is away from organized religion and back to individual spirituality. The shift moves away from right and wrong to love and light, from righteousness to gentleness, from being right to doing the right thing—the kind thing.

It's already happening all over the world. Little acts of kindness. Little steps of tolerance, accepting what was once unacceptable, embracing our differences as well as our same-ness. Loving everyone, refusing to see anyone as unlovable. Praying for peace, being the change we want to see, finding peace within and sharing it with others.

The Healing Balm of Laughter: A good friend once said to me, "If you can laugh at it, you can live with it." In an interview Barbara Walters conducted with the Dalai Lama, what impressed me about His Holiness was how often he laughed. He was as jolly as Santa Claus. A holy man with such a great sense of humor is a nice change of pace from the religious leaders who take their work, and themselves, so seriously.

If common sense fails to bridge the chasm of religious faiths, perhaps humor will. When we develop the ability to laugh at ourselves and find humor in everything, then, as my friend said, "…we can live with it." We can live with our religious differences.

We laugh at everything else, why not at ourselves and ultra-serious religious beliefs? I don't think The Divine laughs at us, but no doubt the Ultimate Being laughs with us. Who, if not The Divine, created humor and laughter? I recall when my children were young and played "Grown-up." They set aside their usual play and became serious, mimicking the way the grown-ups acted. I smiled and laughed, but my laughter was more toward myself and the silly way I must have looked in their eyes.

Likewise, we can take a step back and see our lives in the light of the way The Divine sees us. When we talk about religion we become serious, somber at times, and I wonder if it doesn't cause The Divine to smile at the way we portray what we think spiritual/religious behavior should be. When we squabble and fight like little children I wonder if The Divine doesn't shake His head, chuckle, and wonder, *When will they ever learn?* Laughing at someone can be cruel, but this is not the type of laughter we're considering. We reflect on the healthy laughter that lightens our mood and shines light on our path.

One of the best things that could happen to religious organizations would be for them to develop an institutional sense of humor. They like to make rules, why not make it mandatory for their flock to laugh at least six times a day. And if you fail to meet the quota, your penance would be to watch *I Love Lucy* reruns, or *Seinfeld* episodes.

Perhaps I'm being too hard on religion. Sorry. But, it's time to take a lesson from the Dalai Lama and chuckle, laugh, and enjoy life. I believe religion has the greatest potential and opportunity to create the change that will move us into greater love and understanding. But, with or without the cooperation of religion, change is upon us, and spirituality is lighting the road home.

Chapter 14
INDIVIDUAL WORSHIP

"The progress of the world can certainly never come at all save by the modified action of the individual beings who compose the world."

–George Eliot

A Congregation of One: Church, synagogue, temple, mosque: all bring to mind buildings where individuals go to worship. It may seem ludicrous to propose that these terms, as defined by the gathering of membership, could be held in private. I won't squabble over terms. I'll simply redefine this one to suit my needs. Individual worship, ceremonies, services—whatever term we are comfortable with—can and are being held by individuals.

The thirteen-step concept presented in this work was patterned after twelve-step programs. Why mess with success. Some tweaking was done. We modified the steps to fit the subject matter. But, the overall experience was setup to mimic a successful pattern. We now introduce a minor difference.

The thirteen-step program of Religious Recovery was also set up to work for the individual who, for whatever reason, doesn't feel comfortable in a group setting. Just as I believe religious gathering/worship/spiritual enlightenment can be done alone, I believe healing from religious abuse can be accomplished by any individual who is willing to make the effort. Some may find the group setting the quickest route to recovery, but for others the do-it-yourself home-study kit works best.

Simple Steps to Renewal: Following the thirteen-steps of Religious Recovery provides one road to healing. Once healing is undertaken, we offer a few simple steps for guidance. Yes, you may choose any religious path that feels right to you, but along any path that you choose, we offer these reminders.

Do Unto Others: The golden rule applies to all roads. Buddhists call it karma. What you give out, you receive. Whatever title or name you give, the principle remains the same: do unto others as you want them to do unto you. Treat your brothers and sisters with respect. Show no favoritism, for all are creations of Divine Spirit.

Tolerate and Accept: Remembering that we are all family, we learn to tolerate our differences. Going deeper, we accept our differences as the things that make us unique, special, and fascinating. Instead of letting our differences separate us and pull us into conflict, we celebrate our differences and appreciate the fact that we can learn from each other.

Forgive: I make mistakes—way too many. But, you make mistakes, too. As with the golden rule, I forgive your mistakes, and I hope you will forgive mine. When we forgive, we receive. When we receive, we give. The circle envelops each and all of us in love.

Love and Embrace: We repeat what was said in an earlier chapter because it's important. Tolerance, acceptance, and forgiveness clear the way to embrace and love. The goal of religious belief is love. The essence of The Divine is love.

One word of caution is in order. Love can masquerade itself as religious deception. Love is such an attractive quality that people have been led into toxic systems such as we described with Jim Jones and the "Peoples Temple." The quickest determination of deception is exclusivity. If the religious entity loves only its followers and is fearful of all others, be wary. Apply the tests of tolerance and acceptance. Do they accept other paths or do they believe they are the only true believers. Always remember: "God is too big to fit into one religion."

Meditate, Contemplate, and Pray: These three spiritual practices form the foundation of spiritual observance. Practice them. Put them to use. Listen for direction, and learn to discern the difference between Divine Voice and your ego. Read spiritual books from all faiths as well as books that are not specifically religious—*Cry, The Beloved Country* by Alan Paton and *To Kill a Mockingbird* by Harper Lee come to mind.

Follow Your Path: Find the road that takes you home. Make it your path. Listen to the voices of the Masters who have gone before, but remember that they followed the inner voice of The Divine GPS which told them when and where to turn. And, when they missed a turn, The Divine gently nudged them in the right direction.

Chapter 15

GOING HOME

*"God is at home, it's we who
have gone out for a walk."*
—Meister Eckhart

As a child living at home with my parents and brothers, I didn't appreciate home until we were gone for a period of time. Every summer we packed the car and drove from Cincinnati to Big Stone Gap, Virginia, to visit my maternal grandmother, great grandmother, and other friends and relatives in the area.

Dad grew up in coal mining country on the other side of Black Mountain. After we visited Mom's people, we crossed the mountain, occasionally stopping at the top to admire the view. Getting back in the car, we crossed the state line and passed into Kentucky as we snaked our way to the bottom. Tires screamed as my dad—accustomed to the road he had driven hundreds of times when he courted Mom—sped around hairpin turns. We begged him to slow down.

By the end of the week, our adventure had grown old, and we were ready to head home. With no interstate highways in those days, our trip took eight to ten hours. Patience was not a virtue three restless boys possessed.

Finally, after three hundred "Are we there yet?" questions, half a dozen restroom breaks, and forty threats that started with, "Don't make me stop this car," we topped a hill in northern Kentucky and we finally saw the Ohio River and the Cincinnati skyline.

I looked for that skyline. I loved seeing the tall buildings and the bridge that would lead home. We still had about thirty minutes before pulling into our driveway, but we were close.

When we finally made it home, I sighed. It was still there. Still standing strong and warm and inviting. The trip had tired us, and we wanted to enter and relax, sleep in our own beds, rise to the familiar sounds of the house, and return to family life. The house had not changed, or moved, or disappointed us in any way.

I love Meister Eckhart's quote: *"God is at home, it's we who have gone out for a walk."* We are the ones who have left home. We are on a spiritual adventure. A journey on this planet to explore the wonderful things provided. Deep within, however, lurks a sense that we have left our real home. We are on vacation. Away from the intimate presence of Divine Spirit as we once knew it. In our hearts we know that once this adventure ends, we will return to where we began. To home, and to Love.

God is home. We are in the process of going back to Him. It's been a fun journey, but the reunion will be greater for having been away. We are children of the Divine Supreme Being. He will not let His children lose their way.

I'm tired, and I'm heading home. "Are we there yet?" the question comes again for the three-hundred-and-first time. No, not yet. But soon. Not much longer. Soon we'll see familiar scenes and know the journey is almost over. We'll know it in our hearts. And when we arrive, all we'll want to do is rest, relax, and sleep for a long, long time. I'm looking forward to it, and ...

I'll see you at home.

The Thirteen Steps of Religious Recovery[17]

1) We recognized we were hurt, disappointed, or abused by religion or the religious.

2) Come to believe that The Divine has no religion, is greater than religion, and can heal us from our hurts.

3) Recognize that we are spiritual beings and decide to turn our lives over to "that which is greater than self" referred to in these steps as "The Divine."

4) Accept that this Higher Power is understood in different ways and by different names in various religions and cultures, and open our lives to hearing the Divine Voice in any way it chooses to communicate to us.

5) Share our struggles with others of like-mindedness trusting our anonymity will be guarded by all.

6) Take inventory of ourselves to discover any way in which we have hurt, disappointed, or abused anyone by our religious beliefs.

7) Choose to forgive those who hurt us in the name of religion.

8) Seek forgiveness from those we hurt unless doing so would cause further harm.

9) Forgive ourselves for all harm we may have caused, even if it was well-intended.

10) Seek tolerance, and when possible accept all religious faiths without judgment.

11) Seek through prayer, meditation, and contemplation to improve our relationship with The Divine, praying for clarity of mind, an open heart, and further ways to heal ourselves and our world from the abuses of religion.

12) Having recognized the difference between religion and spirituality, we strive to be true to the Spirit within all of Divine Creation and to be a Light to point the way.

13) We follow the principle that when the student is ready, the teacher will appear. The witness of our lives is the only message we need to carry to others.

---

[17] The Thirteen Steps of Religious Recovery, though inspired by the Twelve Steps of A.A., are not an adaptation. Rather, they were created specifically for this organization, and should not be construed otherwise. A.A. is a program concerned only with recovery from alcoholism. A.A. is a spiritual program, A.A. is not a religious program. Thus, A.A. is not affiliated or allied with any sect, denomination, or specific religious belief.

The Thirteen Stones of Religious Recovery

Spiritual growth is a destination achieved by an active process. For that reason we use active verbs to highlight the twelve stones.

1) **Assert:** I assert that I am responsible for my own spiritual path.

2) **Open:** I partake of spiritual wisdom and knowledge from a variety of sources and open myself to different insights.

3) **Question:** I question every experience, all information, personal motives— mine and others—including the ideas presented by Religious Recovery.

4) **Discern:** It is my responsibility to discern what works for me and what does not, always remembering that what may not resonate with me today may resonate at another time.

5) **Connect:** Not only will I try to discern through mental activity, but I will also discern by connecting with The Divine through prayer, meditation, and contemplation.

6) **Be:** Letting go of past hurts, disappointments and abuses, and letting go of future plans and expectations, I resolve to live in the present moment and simply be. Be present, be open, be available, be with Higher Self.

7) **Feel:** I allow myself to feel. My emotions are part of my being. By allowing myself to feel, I heal and grow.

8) **Release:** After experiencing all feelings, I release any emotions I deem harmful to my spiritual path.

9) **Transform:** By changing my thoughts, I transform my life. I choose to change my thoughts concerning past experiences that hold me in pain. I choose to see them from a higher perspective.

10) **Harmonize:** I look for the harmony in all spiritual belief systems and seek to add my voice to the music of the Earth. I seek peace with all people and with myself.

11) **Laugh:** I choose laughter as the notes of my song. This temporal life is a journey to be enjoyed. I look for the comedy in situations, and I learn to laugh at my own comedy of errors.

12) **Thank:** I am grateful. Gratitude helps me bring out the positive in my life and

also makes room for The Divine to bring additional positive situations, people, and spiritual experiences into my life. I thank those who have guided me on my path.

13) **Love:** I learn to deepen my ability to love when I learn to tolerate, accept, embrace, and forgive. I choose to employ these attributes to my spiritual walk, to my personal relationships, and to my world view.

Additional Reading

This book and its companion works were designed to help facilitate healing at home, in a group, or on retreats. These works are certainly not exhaustive or extensive, and this glossary of other titles was added in the hope that one or more of the titles may be helpful. One author in particular approaches this subject from a Christian viewpoint: *Why Did Jesus, Moses, the Buddha, and Mohammed Cross the Road?: Christian Identity in a Multi-Faith World,* by Brian D. McLaren. Although this is the only title I've listened to by Brian McLaren, he seems to be leading the way of Christian tolerance. He may be one of the few writing about it, but the crowd of those encouraging religious tolerance is growing.

Titles printed by Religious Recovery Press

Why Did Jesus, Moses, the Buddha, and Mohammed Cross the Road?: Christian Identity in a Multi-Faith World, by Brian D. McLaren

Take Back Your Life: Recovering from Cults and Abusive Relationships, by Janja Lalich and Madeleine Tobias

Crisis of Conscience, Abridged for E-Reader Devices, by Raymond Franz [out of print but you can download an abridged copy from Amazon]

Jesus and Lao Tzu: The Parallel Sayings, edited by Martin Aronson

Jesus and Buddha: The Parallel Sayings, edited by Marcus Borg

Jesus, Buddha, Krishna, and Lao Tzu: The Parallel Sayings, by Richard Hooper

Return to the Sacred: Ancient Pathways to Spiritual Awakening, by Jonathan H. Ellerby, Ph.D.

Celebration of Discipline, by Richard Foster

Bhagavad Gita for Beginners: The Song of God in Simplified Prose, [Kindle Edition] by Edward Viljoen

A Course in Miracles, by Helen Schucman

A New Earth: Awakening to Your Life's Purpose, by Eckhart Tolle

The Power of Now: A Guide to Spiritual Enlightenment, by Eckhart Tolle

Living the Wisdom of the Tao: The Complete Tao Te Ching and Affirmations, by Dr. Wayne W. Dyer

How to Run a Religious Recovery Meeting[18]

All Religious Recovery groups are autonomous, and as such, there is no specific way to lead a meeting except as established by individual gatherings, but a few suggestions might make for a smoother experience. Individual meetings attempt through trial and error to find what works best for their gatherings, keeping in mind the fluidity of life and the need for flexibility.

Moderators: Leaders may be used to oversee the meetings, but the moderator does not dominate the group. He/She allows others to speak and does not have to voice a comment after every speaker. The moderator does not need to share more than anyone else in the group, and in fact, may speak less.

Silence: Many people feel uncomfortable when a lull in sharing occurs. Silence should be viewed as a time to reflect on what has been said, and a time to consider whether or not you want to share with the group. No one need feel pressure to share. However, if silence continues for about 45 seconds, the moderator might want to pose a question to the group, or briefly share a personal experience. Listen to your inner guidance and do what feels right to you.

Theme Meetings: Meetings are open to any Religious Recovery topic or theme, and quite often these themes are pulled from the thirteen steps, thirteen stones, and other Religious Recovery suggested readings.

---

[18] This material may be reproduced for use by Religious Recovery meetings. This material is also posted at www.ReligiousRecovery.org

Reading of the Thirteen Steps and/or Thirteen Stones: Some meetings may choose to read the "Thirteen Steps," or the "Thirteen Stones." This can be done by one individual, as a group, or by taking turns reading one step/stone at a time.

Donations: Religious Recovery is **not** at this time a non-profit organization. Donations are accepted to cover the cost of expenses, but donations are **not** tax deductible. We will apply for non-profit status soon and will update the web site accordingly. Excess funds not needed to support the local meeting may be contributed to the Religious Recovery parent group to cover expenses such as the cost of literature, advertising, and space rental.

Opening/Closing: There is no formal way to open or close a meeting. We do not recommend the reading of Scripture — such as The Lord's Prayer taken from Christianity — unless other meetings use something similar from other world religions. The concept of inclusiveness is at play, and to use a reading from only one world faith excludes all others. Generic opening/closings may be used so long as care is taken to offend no one and be at peace with all. I've written sample statements I hope will not offend anyone, but please feel free to formulate your own. If you do, I'd like to encourage you to send me a copy at Wayne@ReligiousRecovery.org.

Suggested Opening: "I am part of Divine creation. I honor all my brothers and sisters. I honor their roads and their beliefs, and will endeavor to share loving acceptance with all I meet. As we share our journeys, we learn from one another. May The Divine guide us and always be at our side."

Suggested Closing: "We are the children of love. Let us love our brothers and sisters, here and everywhere."

Slogans: As the program grows, slogans will emerge to meet the need for concise pieces of advice. But, here are a few that might prove helpful.

Modified Serenity Prayer: "Divine Spirit, grant me the serenity to accept the people I cannot change, the courage to change the one I can, and the wisdom to know that one is me." –author unknown.

"Leave your religion at the Door."

Modified Twelve-Step Slogans:

1) "Take what resonates with you and release what no longer leads you home."

2) "If religion fails, return to spirituality. It will lead you home."

Anonymity: The concept of anonymity should be addressed, especially when visitors are present. Attendees are encouraged to use first names, initials, or pen names. The use of titles such as reverend, pastor, priest, shaman, or monk, are also discouraged. Naming specific religious gatherings, denominations, or world religions is generally avoided.

Cross-Talk: Someone may attend a meeting with a situation in which they feel a need for an immediate answer. The tendency of the group may be to solve the problem, but care needs to be taken not to overwhelm the individual. Giving specific advice is strongly discouraged. Speak from the first person using "I," "me," or "my" statements and avoid "you," "your," or "we" comments. Avoid eye contact and simply share your story and the things you found to be helpful.

Because communication is more than the words we say, be careful to avoid offensive body language such as rolling the eyes, shrugging, dismissive glances, or touching someone. If you need to, keep your eyes focused on your lap, or if seated around a table, focus on a spot on the table.

Sometimes things don't resonate with people because they're not in a place to receive the message, or the message simply doesn't apply to their particular situation. At all times we want to create a safe atmosphere. Do not judge, condemn, or guilt another verbally, mentally, or emotionally.

The golden rule is our guide when it comes to crosstalk. Our modified version states: "Treat others as you would have them treat you."

Further reading describing the importance of the "No Crosstalk" rule can be found at the Co-Dependents Anonymous (CoDA) web site: http://www.codawa.org/literature-docs/literature-docs-wa/crosstalk_statement.htm.

Humor: Laughter is encouraged at meetings. Humor has healing qualities that promote participation and a light-hearted approach. "If you can laugh at it, you can live with it." Remember, we don't laugh at individuals but with them. Learning to laugh at ourselves and our situations brings healing laughter into play.

Newcomer's Guidelines

Relax, take it easy, and enjoy your experience. You are welcome to participate in the meeting, but don't feel obligated. We may be traveling different paths, but we believe our destination is the same. We hope to learn from each other, grow together, and avoid the pitfalls along the way. Welcome to the journey.

What to Expect: Each group develops a format that meets the needs of its participants. Because Religious Recovery meetings are autonomous, you might find different things occurring at different meetings, so here is a list of things you might—or might not—discover.

Someone usually volunteers to serve as a moderator for the meeting. Moderators may read an opening and/or invite those present to read along. They usually introduce themselves and often invite those present to do the same using first names, initials, or pen names only. They may go over these guidelines, or a different set of guidelines created specifically for their group. A reading of the thirteen steps and/or the thirteen stones might be given.

A topic for the gathering may be introduced or the meeting may be open to any subject. Most meetings last about an hour. An opportunity to donate may be presented, but this is strictly voluntary. No membership dues are required and no suggested donation amounts are given. If participants wish to support the work of Religious Recovery, we ask that they do so willingly.

A closing may also be read, and participants can be invited to join hands and repeat it together.

Laughter is not mandatory, but highly encouraged.

A Final Word (or two) from the Author

I am pro religion.

I hope that came through. Much of what you've read reflects my own journey. I'm not perfect, and my decision to share suggests I'm struggling to find my way. I wrote not as an expert, but as a fellow traveler. If you want someone to tell you exactly what to do, when to do it, and how to do it, then this book probably wasn't for you.

I don't want to be a spiritual guru—and I doubt that will ever be a possibility. If I came across as too preachy or authoritarian, I apologize. I wanted you to think for yourself and discover your own way home. Maybe some of my words opened your eyes to angels in disguise, to roads that have grown over from lack of traffic, or to spiritual practices you may have overlooked. Forgive me, too, if I picked on Christianity too much. Because I was born into a Christian family, it's the religious path I know best. You might also feel that some of the writing doesn't support the claim that I'm pro religion, but it's true.

All of a sudden, I feel as if I'm a pimple-faced teenager again, thinking up every possible reason why a girl wouldn't want to go out with me, and remembering how, when I finally screwed up enough courage to approach a girl, I'd say, "You wouldn't want to go out with me, would you?"

I feel like that pimple-faced kid again, except this time I'm not seeking a date with a girl, but a date with a reader. I began with the same mistakes I made years ago, I'm not an expert, I'm struggling to find my path, I'm apologizing now in case I sounded too preachy or too negative about religion.

But, I hope you discovered my approach refreshing. I've heard plenty of religious authorities try to pound their beliefs into the heads of their listeners. I want to whisper in your ear, "Maybe they're right, but maybe they're wrong. Ponder for yourself, and then tell me what you think. Maybe they're a little right and a little wrong. Not everything in life is black or white."

Let me expand on my earlier statement; I am pro religion but I'm even more pro spirituality. At times it seems religion and spirituality oppose each another. That needn't be the case. Spirituality is personal; religion is communal.

Can a person be spiritual without being religious? Absolutely. Can a person be religious without being spiritual? Unfortunately, that answer is also yes. Given the choice, I prefer spirituality over religion. In an ideal world, we can have both. One can complement the other, which was one of the goals of this book.

But, perhaps the main goal of the book was to help you heal from religious abuse and to broaden the view of religion to one of greater understanding—an understanding that there is more than one path that leads home. All roads home are fraught with challenges. When we refute the paths of others, we alienate them from the help we can offer—and also the help we can receive from them.

Therefore, I set out three goals for this book, not necessarily in order of importance to show that:

1   Religion and spirituality can work together.

2.   Healing from religious abuse can be accomplished through spirituality.

3.   All paths lead to The Divine.

I used the expression "The Divine" to represent that which is greater than self, beyond self, eternal, and nameless. Though The Divine is nameless, we have given it many names in order to know—to some degree—what or who we are talking about. Some call it God, the "I am," Buddha, Allah, The Great Spirit, Eternal Life Force, Holy Spirit, Divine Spirit, Mother Earth, and so on. Some are offended by the word God because they believe it only refers to the Christian deity. Those who grew up in a western culture may be offended by the names of Hindu gods or Allah or the ways in which American Indians referred to the elements as gods, but they need to remember that the references may be to the same deity.

Gandhi said, and I believe, "God has no religion."

Though it may have appeared we were heading in different, even opposite directions, I hope you can see we are all trying to reach the same place—home. I wish you peace, joy, and love on your journey.

Let's share our hopes and dreams. Let's share any help or guidance we acquire on our trip.

Let's make peace, do no harm, and play nice together.

I wish you only the best as you awaken to your most fabulous adventure.

For information about Religious Recovery
visit our web site at

www.ReligiousRecovery.org

www.ingramcontent.com/pod-product-compliance
Lightning Source LLC
Chambersburg PA
CBHW051733040426
42447CB00008B/1104